## SERIES TITLES

This Zak Books edition was published in 2009. Zak Books is an imprint of McRae Books Srl.

ASIAN AND AFRICAN EMPIRES

was created and produced by McRae Books Srl
Via del Salviatino 1 — 50016 — Fiesole (Florence) Italy
info@mcraebooks.com
www.mcraebooks.com

Publishers: Anne McRae, Marco Nardi
Series Editor: Anne McRae
Author: Neil Morris
Main Illustrations: Lorenzo Cecchi p. 27; Francesca d'Ottavi pp. 36-37, 38-39, 40-41; Giacinto Gaudenzi pp. 8-9b, 10-11b, 12-13b, 20-21; MM comunicazione (M. Cappon, V. Grimaldi, M. Favilli, G. Sbragi, C. Scutti) pp. 16-17b, 22-23b, 28-29b; Sergio pp. 32-33; Studio Stalio (Alessandro Cantucci, Fabiano Fabbrucci, Andrea Morandi, Ivan Stalio) pp. 43c.
Illustrations: Studio Stalio (Alessandro Cantucci, Fabiano Fabbrucci, Andrea Morandi, Ivan Stalio)
Maps: Paola Baldanzi
Photos: Bridgeman Art Library, London pp. 6-7b, 14–15, 19, 24–25, 44–45b; Lonely Planet Images pp. 34–35b (Brent Winebrenner); ©Photo RMN pp. 30–31b (Michel Urtado).
Art Director: Marco Nardi
Layouts: Starry Dogs Books Ltd.
Project Editor: Loredana Agosta
Research: Lucy Turner Voakes, Loredana Agosta
Editing: Tall Tree Ltd, London
Repro: Litocolor, Florence

Consultants:

Dr. Gregory Possehl is an anthropological archeologist with broad interests in the development of urbanization in the Old World. His specific research and writing have focused on the first phase of urbanization in South Asia, namely in the ancient cities of Mohenjo-Daron and Harappa. He has been conducting field research and excavations in India since 1979.

Library of Congress Cataloging-in-Publication Data

Asian and African Empires
 ISBN 9788860981769

2009923555

Printed and bound in Malaysia.

# HISTORY

# Asian and African Empires

## Neil Morris

Consultant: Dr. Gregory Possehl, Professor of Archeology, Department of Anthropology, University of Pennsylvania and Curator of the Asian Section, University of Pennsylvania Museum of Archeology and Anthropology.

Zak BOOKS

# Contents

*A decorative turban pin made for the Moghul emperor Shah Jahan (reigned 1628–58).*

# TIMELINE

| | 1350 | 1400 | 1450 | 1500 |
|---|---|---|---|---|
| **AFRICA** | | | | Reign of Songhai ruler Askia the Great. |
| | | | Dogon peoples migrate to plateau region near the Niger River. | The armies of Ottoman Sultan Suleiman I conquer northern Africa. |
| **THE OTTOMANS, SAFAVIDS AND UZBEKS** | | | | The Uzbek confederacy is formed. |
| | | | | Reign of Safavid founder Ismail I. |
| | | | | Reign of Ottoman Suleiman the Magnificent. |
| **INDIA** | | | Life of Guru Nanak, founder of Sikhism. | Babur founds the Mughal Empire. |
| | | | | Adil Shahi Dynasty founded in Bijapur sultanate. |
| | | | | Reign of Krishna Deva Raya, great ruler of Vijayanagar. |
| **CHINA** | The Ming Dynasty is founded. | Building of the Forbidden City. Ming capital moves from Nanjing to Beijing. | Mongol invasions lead to further extension of the Great Wall. | A Portuguese ship carries the first Europeans to reach China by sea. |
| | | Reign of Xuande, a great patron of the arts. | | |
| **JAPAN** | Ashikaga Yoshimitsu rules as shogun, moving his administration to Muromachi in 1378. | | Ashikaga Yoshimasa rules as shogun. | |
| **KOREA** | | Koryo Dynasty is overthrown; the Chosôn Dynasty takes power. | Development of the modern Korean alphabet is completed. | |
| | | Reign of Sejong, early Chosôn culture reaches its height. | | |
| **SOUTHEAST ASIA** | The city of Ayutthaya is founded. | Thai forces capture Angkor, and the Khmer abandon the city. | Reign of King Trailok of Ayutthaya (Thailand), during which there are continuous wars with Cambodia. | Portuguese traders arrive in Ayutthaya. |
| | | | Reign of Burmese queen Shin Sawbu at Pegu; trade flourishes. | Tabinshwehti of the Toungoo Dynasty, unifies Burma. |

# Introduction

This book covers the history of the civilizations, empires, and kingdoms of Asia and Africa from the early 15th to the late 18th century. Powerful empires fought for dominance in Asia, including Muslim sultanates in the west and the great Ming Dynasty that ruled for nearly three hundred years in the Far East. The long line of Ming emperors finally gave way to neighboring Manchus, who succeeded in making the Chinese empire even bigger. The influence of Chinese culture was felt strongly in Japan and Korea, but Japanese emperors lost authority and real power passed into the hands of noble warlords. African kingdoms were smaller than those of Asia. During this period their rulers came under pressure from Muslim invaders in the north and European explorers and traders along the west coast. In both Africa and Asia, different religions and European ambitions had great influence on the civilizations they touched.

*A late 17th-century enamelled teapot from China.*

*Black wooden figurine of the founder hero of the Luba Empire in south-central Africa.*

*Portrait of Ottoman sultan Mehmed II, who conquered Byzantine Constantinople in 1453.*

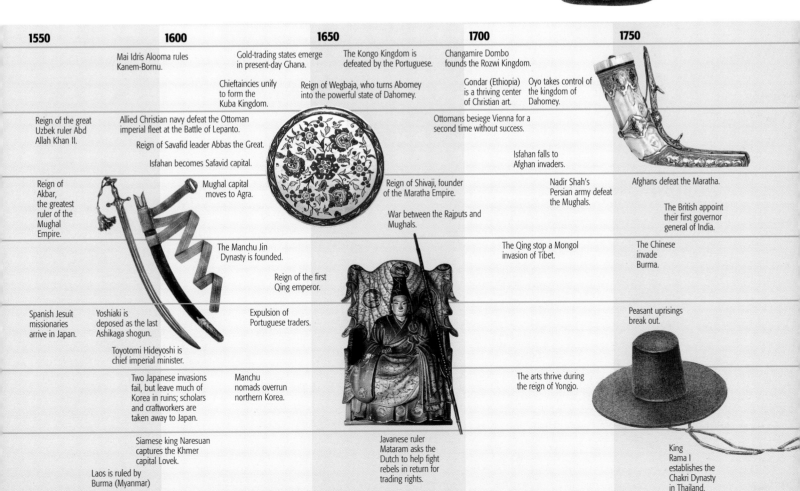

| 1550 | 1600 | 1650 | 1700 | 1750 |
|---|---|---|---|---|
| | Mai Idris Alooma rules Kanem-Bornu. | Gold-trading states emerge in present-day Ghana. | The Kongo Kingdom is defeated by the Portuguese. | Changamire Dombo founds the Rozwi Kingdom. |
| | | Chieftaincies unify to form the Kuba Kingdom. | Reign of Wegbaja, who turns Abomey into the powerful state of Dahomey. | Gondar (Ethiopia) is a thriving center of Christian art. / Oyo takes control of the kingdom of Dahomey. |
| Reign of the great Uzbek ruler Abd Allah Khan II. | Allied Christian navy defeat the Ottoman imperial fleet at the Battle of Lepanto. | | Ottomans besiege Vienna for a second time without success. | |
| | Reign of Safavid leader Abbas the Great. | | | |
| | Isfahan becomes Safavid capital. | | Isfahan falls to Afghan invaders. | |
| Reign of Akbar, the greatest ruler of the Mughal Empire. | Mughal capital moves to Agra. | Reign of Shivaji, founder of the Maratha Empire. | Nadir Shah's Persian army defeat the Mughals. | Afghans defeat the Maratha. |
| | | War between the Rajputs and Mughals. | | The British appoint their first governor general of India. |
| | The Manchu Jin Dynasty is founded. | | The Qing stop a Mongol invasion of Tibet. | The Chinese invade Burma. |
| | | Reign of the first Qing emperor. | | |
| Spanish Jesuit missionaries arrive in Japan. | Yoshiaki is deposed as the last Ashikaga shogun. | Expulsion of Portuguese traders. | | Peasant uprisings break out. |
| | Toyotomi Hideyoshi is chief imperial minister. | | | |
| | Two Japanese invasions fail, but leave much of Korea in ruins; scholars and craftworkers are taken away to Japan. | Manchu nomads overrun northern Korea. | The arts thrive during the reign of Yongjo. | |
| | Siamese king Naresuan captures the Khmer capital Lovek. | Javanese ruler Mataram asks the Dutch to help fight rebels in return for trading rights. | | King Rama I establishes the Chakri Dynasty in Thailand. |
| | Laos is ruled by Burma (Myanmar) | | | |

# Kingdoms and Empires

**M**any civilizations became established and developed in Africa and Asia during the period from 1400–1800. Some declined and even collapsed during the period, and others were overrun by invaders or absorbed by other empires. There was often conflict between neighboring powers, as ruling dynasties vied for control. Religious missionaries and ambitious traders traveled across the continents, spreading their beliefs and cultural traditions.

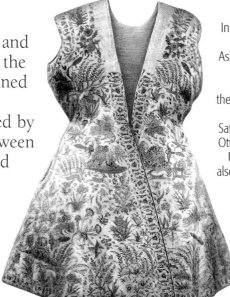

## Muslim Empires

In the early 16th century four Muslim powers dominated west and south Asia—the Ottomans, Safavids, Uzbeks, and Mughals. In 1517 the Ottoman Turks gained control of Egypt and then expanded their empire along the coastal region of North Africa. The Safavids, who were Shiite rivals to the Ottomans, united tribes in Persia. The Uzbek confederation of central Asia also fought the Safavids and Mughals, who moved down to the Indian subcontinent in search of new territory.

*An embroidered muslin hunting jacket of the Mughal emperor Jahangir (reigned 1605–27).*

*Portrait of the Ottoman sultan Selim II (reigned 1566–74) wearing his feathered royal turban.*

## Far-Eastern Dynasties

The largest and dominant empire of the Far East was China, which was ruled by two great imperial dynasties—the Ming (1368–1644) and the Qing (1644–1912). They had a great influence on the rulers and cultures of Korea and Japan, where noble warlords exercised real power.

*A mounted bowman of the Manchu, who formed the Qing Dynasty of China.*

## African Kingdoms

Between the 16th and 18th centuries, important kingdoms came to power in Sub-Saharan Africa. Some were successful and grew, while Islam spread down the east coast from North Africa. South of the Congo River in central Africa, several Bantu-speaking kingdoms developed, including those of the Luba and Lunda peoples. In the southeast, the territory of the Mwenemutapa Kingdom eventually became part of the Rozwi Empire.

*An Akan ceremonial sword (from present-day Ghana). The handle was made of wood covered with gold leaf.*

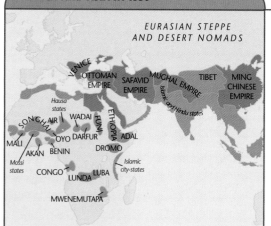

### AFRICA AND ASIA IN 1530

*EURASIAN STEPPE AND DESERT NOMADS*

VENICE
OTTOMAN EMPIRE
SAFAVID EMPIRE
MUGHAL EMPIRE
*Islamic and Hindu states*
TIBET
MING CHINESE EMPIRE
Hausa states
SONGHAI
AIR
WADAI
FUNJ
ETHIOPIA
OYO
DARFUR
ADAL
MALI
AKAN
BENIN
DROMO
Mossi states
CONGO
LUNDA
LUBA
*Islamic city-states*
MWENEMUTAPA

## Empires

*The map shows the important empires and kingdoms of the two continents around 1530. The Far East was dominated by the largest empire of all, Ming China, while western Asia was split between the Mughals, Safavids, and Ottomans. None of the African kingdoms was as large, and much of the continent did not come under any centralized power.*

*A 16th-century stoneware jar used to hold fresh water during the Japanese tea ceremony.*

*Right: This Sikh emblem contains a ring, a double-edged sword, and two crossed daggers. Sikhism was founded in northern India in the late 15th century.*

## The Role of Religion

The great world religions influenced both the politics and culture of the empires. India was the birthplace of Hinduism and Buddhism, and Buddhist monks took their beliefs to the Far East. Christian missionaries also traveled to Africa and Asia. At the same time, Islam continued to spread from southwest Asia and had a great impact on Africa.

*Above: Self-portrait by Hakuin (1686–1769), who helped revive Zen Buddhism in Japan.*

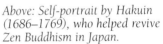

*The Madar-i Shah madrasa in Isfahan (in modern Iran) was built in 1706–14 by the last Safavid ruler.*

*The gold-producing Akan states included Asante. This gold sword ornament takes the form of a fish.*

# Western and Northern Africa

Several important kingdoms and empires developed and expanded in northwest Africa between 1500 and 1800. This meant that most farmers and traders came under the rule of a king and a central government. Some successful empires thrived, but they had to accept the influence of Islam as it spread steadily south from the Mediterranean coast. At the same time, European traders made their way inland from the Atlantic coast in a determined search for gold, ivory, and slaves.

### Yoruba Kingdoms

Yoruba-speaking peoples created several city-states, of which the most powerful were Ife and Oyo. The Oyo Empire was at the height of its power between 1650 and 1750, dominating the region between the Volta River (in present-day Ghana) and the Niger River (in Nigeria). Oyo craftsmen produced stunning works of bronze and terra-cotta, but their kingdom's power began to decline from the mid-1700s.

*This ivory ceremonial sword was carried by a chief of the small Yoruba state of Owo.*

### Magreb States

In the early 16th century the Turkish sea captain Barbarossa helped join the coast of present-day Algeria to the Ottoman Empire. By then Morocco was also ruled by a dynasty of Islamic rulers, and Tunisia became part of the Ottoman Empire in 1574. Muslims controlled the whole of the Maghreb coastal region, from where pirates raided Mediterranean towns and shipping as part of the wars against Spain.

*The kasbah (citadel or fortress) at Telouet, in Morocco. These fortresses acted as residences for local leaders and were used to defend nearby cities.*

## WESTERN AND NORTHERN AFRICA

**1493–1528**
*Reign of Songhai ruler Askia the Great.*

**1520–1566**
*Reign of Ottoman Sultan Suleiman I (the "Lawgiver" or the "Magnificent"), whose armies conquer northern Africa.*

**1580–1617**
*Mai Idris Alooma rules Kanem-Bornu and extends his empire.*

**1591**
*The Songhai are defeated by a Moroccan army in the Battle of Tondibi.*

**1630–1690**
*Denkyira and other Akan gold-trading states emerge in present-day Ghana.*

**c. 1645–1685**
*Reign of Wegbaja, who turns Abomey into the powerful state of Dahomey.*

**1701–1712**
*Reign of Osei Tutu as ruler of Asante, whose territory increases greatly.*

**1724–1748**
*Oyo takes control of the kingdom of Dahomey and demands tribute.*

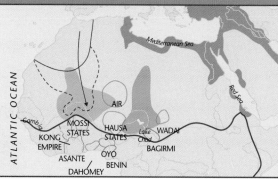

**WESTERN AND NORTHERN AFRICA**

Mediterranean Sea

ATLANTIC OCEAN

Red Sea

AIR

Gambia

MOSSI STATES

KONG EMPIRE

HAUSA STATES

Lake Chad

WADAI

BAGIRMI

ASANTE

OYO

BENIN

DAHOMEY

- Ottoman Empire,
- Kanem Bornu Empire, greatest extent
- Songhai Empire, greatest extent
- - - - Moroccan expansion
→ Moroccan invasion
— Southern limit of Islamic influence

### Empires and Kingdoms

*The Songhai Empire dominated West Africa in the 16th century, until it was attacked by Moroccan invaders. The nearby Kanem-Bornu Empire (north of Lake Chad) was at its greatest around 1600, but then began to decline. The map shows these kingdoms at their greatest extent, as well as the kingdoms of Asante and Oyo. Islamic influence grew during this period.*

## The Dogon Peoples

The Dogon group of peoples migrated north to the plateau region near the Niger River in present-day Mali towards the end of the 15th century. They lived in villages, pressed up against cliffs and hills, where they were safe from invaders. The Dogon mainly lived as farmers, and their craftsmen worked in wood and metal. They believed that a creator god named Amma sent an ark into the world to organize and populate it.

*This Dogon wooden vessel, more than 6.5 feet (2 m) long, represents the original creator's ark.*

## The Dahomey

The Fon people's kingdom of Dahomey, in the south of present-day Benin, was most powerful during the 18th century. It was founded as the smaller Abomey around 1600, and this later became the capital city and a province of the larger kingdom. Dahomey took many captives as the king expanded his boundaries. Some were forced to work as farmers for the royal court or the army, while others were sold as slaves to the Europeans.

*The Dahomey king was protected by a large group of female bodyguards. These warriors, known as Amazons to the Europeans, also served in battle against neighboring kingdoms.*

*This late 17th-century Qur'an shows African influences on the Arabic script.*

# Eastern, Central, and Southern Africa

## TIMELINE

**1527–1543**
*Muslims from neighboring Adal destroy many of Christian Ethiopia's churches, monasteries, and libraries.*

**c. 1625**
*King Shyaam a-Mbul a Ngoong unifies chieftaincies into the Kuba Kingdom.*

**1631**
*Portuguese conquer the Swahili port of Mombasa.*

**1632–1667**
*Reign of Emperor Fasiladas in Ethiopia.*

**1652**
*The Dutch found Cape Colony in the south.*

**1665**
*The Portuguese defeat Kongo at the Battle of Mbwila.*

**c. 1684–1706**
*Life of Kimpa Vita (Dona Beatriz) in the Kongo Kingdom.*

**c. 1690**
*Changamire Dombo conquers territory around the Zambezi River and founds the Rozwi Kingdom.*

**1706**
*Beginning of the chaotic "Age of Princes" in Ethiopia.*

Between the 16th and 18th centuries, large political units also developed in the southern half of Africa. Several states grew up around the great East African lakes, including Rwanda, where Tutsi herdsmen provided leaders who dominated Hutu farming communities. Further south were the large Bantu-speaking states of Lunda and Luba, as well as the kingdoms of Mwenemutapa and Rozwi. Some of these African states fought with each other, and by the end of the period they were all under pressure from European raiders and traders.

— Southern limit of Islamic influence

### Empires and Kingdoms
*From the early 1600s the Bantu-speaking Lunda people had one of the largest and most powerful kingdoms. By the 18th century, some groups had broken away to form their own, smaller empires. Similarly, there were many small kingdoms on the island of Madagascar, including Merina, which was founded toward the end of the 16th century on a central plateau and later expanded.*

### Kongo
Kongo lay in west-central Africa, around the Congo River (across parts of present-day Angola, Congo, and DR Congo). During the 16th century its Bantu-speaking people fell out with the Portuguese, who increased their slaving raids. The kingdom declined, was defeated by the Portuguese in 1665, and broke up into warring chiefdoms. Early in the 18th century, a young Kongolese woman named Kimpa Vita introduced the cult of St. Anthony and tried to stop the cycle of internal wars. She failed and was burned at the stake.

*An 18th-century Kongolese brass pectoral of St. Anthony of Padua. The saint was known as Toni Malau ("Anthony of good fortune").*

*People of the Kuba kingdom wore special masks at dancing ceremonies. The king honored someone else by choosing him to wear the royal mask, which was crowned with a feather headdress.*

*The castle at Gondar was built when the new Ethiopian capital was founded.*

### Ethiopia
The Christian kingdom of Ethiopia was attacked and badly damaged by Muslims during the 16th century. The Ethiopians were finally helped to repel the Muslims by the Portuguese, and in 1632 Emperor Fasiladas moved his capital to Gondar. By 1700 the city was a thriving center of Christian art and scholarship, but by then the empire's central government was in decline. A state of feudal anarchy, dominated by powerful regional warlords, took over from imperial authority.

*Ethiopian wooden statue.*

*This wooden bowl was used by the Venda-speaking people of southern Africa. It was filled with water, to which maize kernels were added for divining purposes.*

## Kuba

The Kuba Kingdom, in the interior of present-day DR Congo in central Africa, was formed in the 17th century from a number of smaller chieftaincies. It was run by the Bushoong people, who brought with them their own artistic and ceremonial traditions. These included wooden helmet masks representing their founding ancestor, Woot, and their king. Kuba craftsmen also worked with copper, iron, and brass, making useful tools and ceremonial weapons.

## Southern States

There were many small states in the southern regions. The Mwenemutapa Kingdom lay between the Zambezi and Limpopo rivers (in present-day Zimbabwe and Mozambique). In the 17th century the state lost power when the Portuguese deposed its king. By the end of the century, the territory was part of the Rozwi Empire, which stretched into present-day Botswana and South Africa.

# The Ottoman Golden Age

The Ottomans were named after their founder and first ruler, Osman (or Uthman, c. 1258–1326). He was the chief of a nomadic Turkic tribe of central Asia that fled from the Mongols and settled in northwest Anatolia (modern Turkey). He and his Muslim successors fought the Christian Byzantines, and after capturing their capital of Constantinople, went on to enjoy a period of great power and importance in the 16th century.

*Selim I (ruled 1512–20) was known as "the Grim" because of the violent way in which he dealt with his rivals.*

### The Sultan's Men

A highly disciplined force of infantrymen acted as the sultan's bodyguards. They were known as Janissaries, or "new troops." The force was originally made up mainly of young Christian prisoners of war from the Balkans. They were given a Muslim education and military training, and were taught to speak Turkish.

*A group of Janissaries in marching order.*

### Sultan's Palace

In the 1460s Mehmed the Conqueror had a sultan's palace built in his new capital, overlooking the Bosphorus. Surrounded by high walls and four courtyards, the Topkapi Palace housed the sultan along with his family, harem, advisers, ministers, and religious officials. More than 4,000 slaves lived within the walls of the palace, which served as the center of government. By the 16th century the palace also housed an imperial art studio and library.

*In this illustration of the Topkapi Palace, the sultan listens in a private room to the deliberations of his ministers.*

### Osman's Successors

The Ottoman rulers fought relentlessly against the Christian Byzantines. Osman's son Murad (ruled 1360–89) captured the Byzantines' second city, Edirne (in modern Turkey). But the greatest prize was claimed in 1453, when the seventh sultan, Mehmed II, captured their first city–Constantinople–and made it the Ottoman capital. The Ottomans renamed the city Istanbul.

*Hagia Sophia, the 6th-century Byzantine Church of Holy Wisdom in Constantinople, was turned into a mosque when the city was taken.*

*The ceremonial monogram of Suleiman the Magnificent.*

### Ottoman Society

The Ottomans called Suleiman I "the Lawgiver," because he reformed the empire's legal system. The ruling class was made up of the imperial family, landowners, military leaders, and religious officials. Everyone else paid taxes to the empire, and craftworkers were members of recognized guilds, which set prices and upheld quality. Mosques served as religious and social centers, but Muslim leaders were generally tolerant of other religions.

*Public baths were an important feature of daily life in the towns, and some were designed by great Ottoman architects. There were separate days for men and women.*

## THE OTTOMAN EMPIRE C. 1640

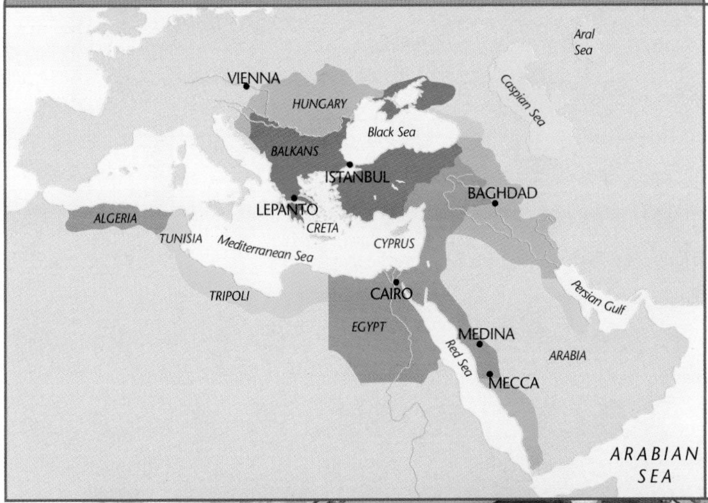

VIENNA
HUNGARY
Aral Sea
Caspian Sea
Black Sea
BALKANS
ISTANBUL
BAGHDAD
LEPANTO
CRETA
ALGERIA
TUNISIA
Mediterranean Sea
CYPRUS
Persian Gulf
TRIPOLI
CAIRO
EGYPT
Red Sea
MEDINA
MECCA
ARABIA
ARABIAN SEA

- 1300–1481
- 1515–1520
- 1520–1566
- 1566–1683

### Growth of the Empire

The Ottoman Empire experienced a golden age in the 16th century during the reign of its tenth ruler, Suleiman I. The empire was at its richest and most powerful, and Suleiman was known as "the Magnificent" in the Western world. He was recognized as a great soldier and administrator. Imperial armies invaded Hungary, Persia, and northern Africa, and the Ottoman navy dominated much of the Mediterranean and Red Seas. The map shows how the empire had expanded by the 17th century.

## THE OTTOMANS

**1444–1446, 1451–1481**
Reign of Mehmed II, named "the Conqueror" after he captured Constantinople.

**1448**
Murad II defeats a Hungarian force led by nobleman John Hunyadi in the Battle of Kosovo.

**1481–1512**
Reign of Bayezid II, during which the empire becomes the leading naval power in the Mediterranean region.

**1517**
Selim I defeats the Mamelukes and gains control of Egypt, Palestine, and Syria, almost doubling the size of the empire.

**1520–1566**
Reign of Suleiman the Magnificent, when the empire reaches its peak.

**1526**
Ottomans capture Belgrade and defeat Hungary at the Battle of Mohacs.

**1529**
Suleiman lays an unsuccessful siege to the Habsburg capital of Vienna.

**1534**
Suleiman takes Baghdad from the Persians.

**1571**
Allied Christian navy of the Holy League defeats the imperial fleet of galleys at the Battle of Lepanto.

# The Ottoman Decline

After the reign of Suleiman the Magnificent, the Ottoman Empire entered a long period of stagnation and then decline. There was corruption in government and among the ruling class, and low pay and high taxes affected workers throughout the empire. Several sultans made attempts to bring in reforms and restore success, but the problems were made worse by military defeats. The imperial army and navy were often still successful, but they lost many important battles, and gradually the empire was forced to give up most of its European lands.

*An Iznik-ware dish.*

## Causes of Decline

In the late 16th century, Dutch and British success in closing international trade routes through the Middle East affected the Ottomans. Their guilds were unable to compete with cheap European goods, so Ottoman industry declined and workers were poorly paid. At the same time taxes were increased, central government became weaker, and there were problems with food supply. Corruption and theft increased, and there were revolts in the provinces.

*A print showing 17th-century Algiers. The Ottomans continued to defend the city by land and sea.*

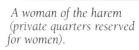

*A woman of the harem (private quarters reserved for women).*

## Ottoman Style

The basic Ottoman clothing style was the long, loose tunic called a caftan, which was worn in variations by both men and women. While women wore a veil or scarf to cover their face, Muslim men wore a white turban. People of high rank favored a large turban, and the imperial family had feather decorations. Christians were denoted by wearing a blue turban, and Jews wore yellow. The town of Iznik (ancient Nicaea) became famous for its beautiful pottery bowls, jugs, and dishes, and later for wall tiles.

*This 18th-century Turkish School painting shows Selim III receiving an ambassador at the Gate of Felicity in the Topkapi Palace.*

### The Tulip Period

The period 1717–30, during the reign of Ahmed III, is called the Tulip Period. The flowers became fashionable in Istanbul at a time when Grand Vizier Ibrahim Pasha encouraged the imperial court to take on a more European style. The period is also associated with an art movement similar to European Rococo, and the paintings of masters such as Abdulcelil Levni used softer colors than previously. The court poet Ahmed Nedim wrote lyrical poems and songs that were full of grace.

*Portrait of Ahmed III by Levni.*

### Warfare

A series of military defeats led to a great loss of territory and power. At the end of the 17th century, a disastrous defeat by an alliance led by Holy Roman Emperor Leopold I led to a great loss of European territory that had been in Ottoman possession for two centuries. This marked the beginning of the Ottoman retreat from Europe, which was hastened by further losses to Austria-Hungary, Russia, and others.

### Reforms

During the 17th and 18th centuries sultans and their ministers tried to restore the government and social systems that had been so successful earlier. Corrupt officials were executed, provincial revolts were put down, new coinage was introduced, and trade and industry were encouraged. Nevertheless, power remained in the hands of a selfish ruling class, and the reforms were only partly successful.

*Turkish pistol case.*

# The Safavids and the Uzbeks

The Safavids were descended from the head of the 13th-century Persian Sufi order of Safawiyah. Their founder proclaimed Shi'ism to be the state religion throughout his empire at the beginning of the 16th century. The Turkic-Mongol Uzbek tribes, who occupied lands to the northeast of the Safavid Empire, were Sunnite Muslims. This religious difference heightened tensions between the hostile neighbors, who vied for territory. By the end of the 17th century, both the Safavid Empire and the Uzbek confederation were in decline.

*Mosaic from the dome of the Lutfallah mosque in Isfahan, completed in 1619.*

## The Safavids

Founding ruler Ismail was first shah of Azerbaijan and then of Persia. Before the end of the 16th century, the greatest Safavid ruler—Abbas I—came to power. He established his imperial capital at Isfahan and turned it into a center of culture, created a standing army to oppose both the Uzbeks and the Ottomans, developed a single coinage, and encouraged trade with Europe and Mughal India. He and his successors also gave new life to Persian art and architecture.

### THE SAFAVID EMPIRE

Black Sea

Caspian Sea

OTTOMAN EMPIRE

MESOPOTAMIA

SAFAVID EMPIRE

Persian Gulf

Red Sea

Arabian Sea

UZBEKS

*This mural detail shows Ismail I stabbing an Ottoman horseman at the Battle of Caldiron, which the Safavids lost. According to legend, Ismail's sword could cut a man in two.*

### Between the Ottomans and the Uzbeks

*The Safavid Empire disputed territory with the Ottomans to the west and the Uzbeks to the northeast. The Safavids won a victory over the Uzbeks in 1510, but four years later were defeated by the Ottomans, which checked their expansion west. There was a continuing struggle with their two rivals, and during the reign of Abbas the Great the Safavids pushed as far as Mesopotamia in the west and Transoxania in the east.*

- ░ Area invaded by Ottoman forces 1514-1638
- ▓ Ottoman Empire before 1514
- ▒ Safavid Empire
- ░ Maximum range of armies of Uzbek khans
- → Major Ottoman campaign
- → Uzbek invasion 1587

## Centers of Trade

The Safavid capital Isfahan and Uzbek Bukhara were both great centers of trade. At Isfahan, a new public square was built in the heart of the city during the 1590s. The square itself was used for ceremonial purposes, and it was also surrounded by two-storied rows of shops. Under the Uzbek Shaybanids, Bukhara replaced Samarkand as the trading hub of Central Asia. The city had large bazaars and a separate horse market.

## The Uzbeks

The first ruling dynasty of the combined Uzbek tribes, the Shaybanids, held power throughout the 16th century. They ruled from their capital of Bukhara (in modern Uzbekistan), where they built mosques and other impressive buildings. The Shaybanid khans were also great patrons of the arts. After their demise, the Uzbek confederation split into three separate khanates—Bukhara (including Samarkand), Khiva (to the northwest), and Kokand (in the Ferghana valley).

## The Last of the Safavids

Decline began to set in after the death of Abbas the Great. Shah Abbas II (reigned 1642–66) ran his government well and succeeded in regaining central authority. But his successors allowed more power to those religious scholars who believed they should have more say in running the state. There was a series of revolts, and in 1722 Shah Husayn was forced to abdicate by invading Afghans.

*Safavid gunpowder flask.*

*Abd Allah Khan II, who expanded Uzbek territory in the late 16th century.*

*The covered bazaars of Bukhara were filled with busy stalls and workshops. Merchants and craftworkers sold local goods as well as produce such as silk imported from the east.*

# Origins of the Mughal

The Mughals (sometimes called Moguls) were named after their Mongol ancestors. They came originally from central Asia, traveling south to the Indian subcontinent at the beginning of the 16th century. The early Mughal rulers continued to follow Islam but were tolerant of other religions. They allowed the subcontinent's Hindu majority to go on following their own culture, creating a blend of Persian and Indian influences. The empire expanded rapidly during the 16th century, and great rulers such as Akbar organized its structure and government well.

*Miniature of Babur, who was an accomplished poet and writer of memoirs as well as a great military leader.*

*A lady of the harem dressing her hair. Mughal leaders and noblemen had more than one wife and often had a large number of children.*

## Founding the Empire

Babur (1483–1530), a Turkic warrior ruler from Ferghana (in present-day Uzbekistan), was descended from two great Mongol leaders, Genghis Khan and Timur. In 1501 he lost Samarkand to one of his greatest opponents, Muhammad Shaybani Khan of the Uzbeks (see page 16). Babur decided to head south, capturing Kabul and Kandahar, and finally his army won a great victory over the sultan of Delhi. This marked the foundation of the Mughal Empire.

*Humayun's tomb in Delhi took nine years to build. It was made of red sandstone and white marble.*

### THE MUGHAL EMPIRE 1561–1687

KABUL
LAHORE
KANDAHAR
HIMALAYAS
DELHI
SIKRI
AGRA
ARABIAN SEA
BAY OF BENGAL
DECCAN

→ Babur's advance 1516-29

Akbar's empire in 1561

The Mughal empire at Akbar's death in 1605

The empire at its peak in 1687

## Civil War and Restoration

In 1539–40 Babur's son Humayun, the second Mughal emperor, was twice defeated in battle by a force of invading Afghan Surs. Humayun was forced to take refuge in Persia, where he received military aid from the Safavid Shah Tahmasp. Having retaken Kandahar and Kabul, Humayun went on to capture Lahore and Delhi, where civil war had broken out. After a gap of 15 years, Humayun resumed his rule in 1555. He died the following year in an accident.

## Imperial Expansion

*Babur's territory was limited to the plain of the Ganges River, and his successors gradually expanded the empire to the west and south. By the time of Akbar's death in 1605, the Mughals controlled the whole of the subcontinent, from the Gulf of Arabia to the Bay of Bengal. Later in the century, the empire stretched much further south into the Deccan and reached its peak.*

## Jahangir

Akbar's son Salim assumed the title of Jahangir ("world conqueror") when he succeeded his father in 1605. Despite rebelling against Akbar during his lifetime, Jahangir adopted many of his father's policies and expanded the empire further. The new ruler's patronage of the arts led to great developments in Mughal painting and music.

*This miniature was commissioned by Jahangir in 1620 to show his dream of friendship with his great rival, Abbas I (on the left). Two years later, Abbas took Kandahar from Jahangir.*

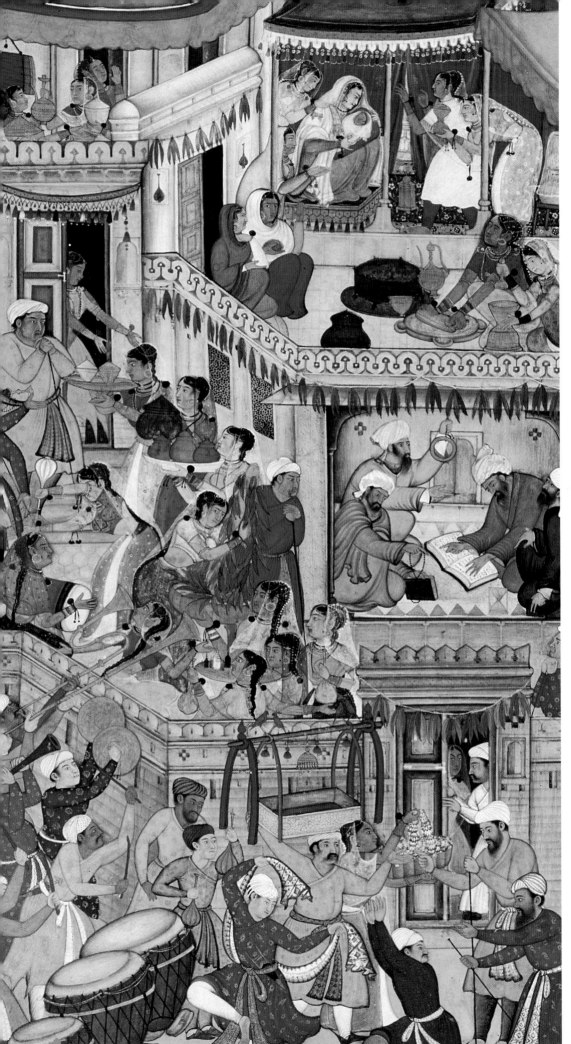

## THE EARLY MUGHAL EMPIRE

**1526**
Babur founds the Mughal Empire.

**1535**
Humayun (ruled 1530–40, 1555–56) invades Gujarat.

**1556–1605**
Reign of Akbar, the greatest ruler of the Mughal Empire.

**1569**
Akbar founds Fatehpur Sikri, near Agra, as his capital.

**1576**
Completion of the conquest of Bengal.

**1598**
Mughal capital moves to Agra.

**1605–27**
Reign of the fourth emperor, Jahangir.

**1614**
Jahangir captures the great Rajput fortress of Rajasthan.

**1622**
The Mughals lose the fortress of Kandahar to Safavid ruler Abbas I after a 45-day siege.

### Akbar

The founder's grandson, Akbar, became ruler at 13. He soon set about expanding Mughal territory, and at the same time set up an effective system for organizing and governing the empire, including new methods of tax collection. Akbar became known for his justice and religious toleration. Despite some resistance from senior orthodox Muslims, his approach won the support and loyalty of many Hindus.

*Akbar's household rejoices at the birth of his second son, Murad. Scene from an illustration accompanying the Akbarnama, a biography written by Abu l-Fadl in the 1590s.*

# The Mughal Decline

The Mughals never recovered their power after the death of their last great emperor, Aurangzeb, early in the 18th century. During his reign the Marathas, a Hindu people from western India, fought the Mughals for territory and succeeded in expanding their own influence. The Marathas themselves had great rivals for power in the Afghans and the British. This left the Mughals with little authority, and by the end of the 18th century, they had no real empire left.

*Silver rupees from Aurangzeb's imperial mint at Surat.*

*A 17th-century Mughal sword.*

### From Peak to Decline

Aurangzeb was the last of the great Mughal emperors. He fought off invasions in the north and expanded the empire to the south. But he created great discontent by executing a Sikh guru, reintroducing a tax on non-Muslims, and destroying Hindu temples. These intolerant acts undid much of his predecessors' work and weakened the Mughals' authority. His reign left the empire with considerable problems and led to its rapid decline.

### Wars of Succession

The Mughal succession was often disputed with great violence. Jahangir's son Khurram had his brothers killed in order to gain the throne as Shah Jahan. His reign was a troubled one, and when he fell ill in 1657, his four sons contested the throne by making war on each other. Aurangzeb emerged the victor, claimed the title and imprisoned his father in the Agra fort. Shah Jahan died there 8 years later.

*This miniature of Shah Jahan on horseback was painted by a court artist. His reign was a golden age of Mughal art and architecture.*

### Mughal Empress

Jahandar Shah's short reign (1712–13) began when he defeated his brothers and ended when he was overthrown by his own nephew. During his time as emperor Jahandar gave his favorite wife Lal Kunwar, who was famous for her beauty and musical skills, a title meaning "chosen of the palace." She acted as an empress and soon made sure that her whole family received special status and favors. Lal Kunwar even accompanied the emperor into battle.

*This 18th-century painting shows a Mughal prince and consort in their palace garden.*

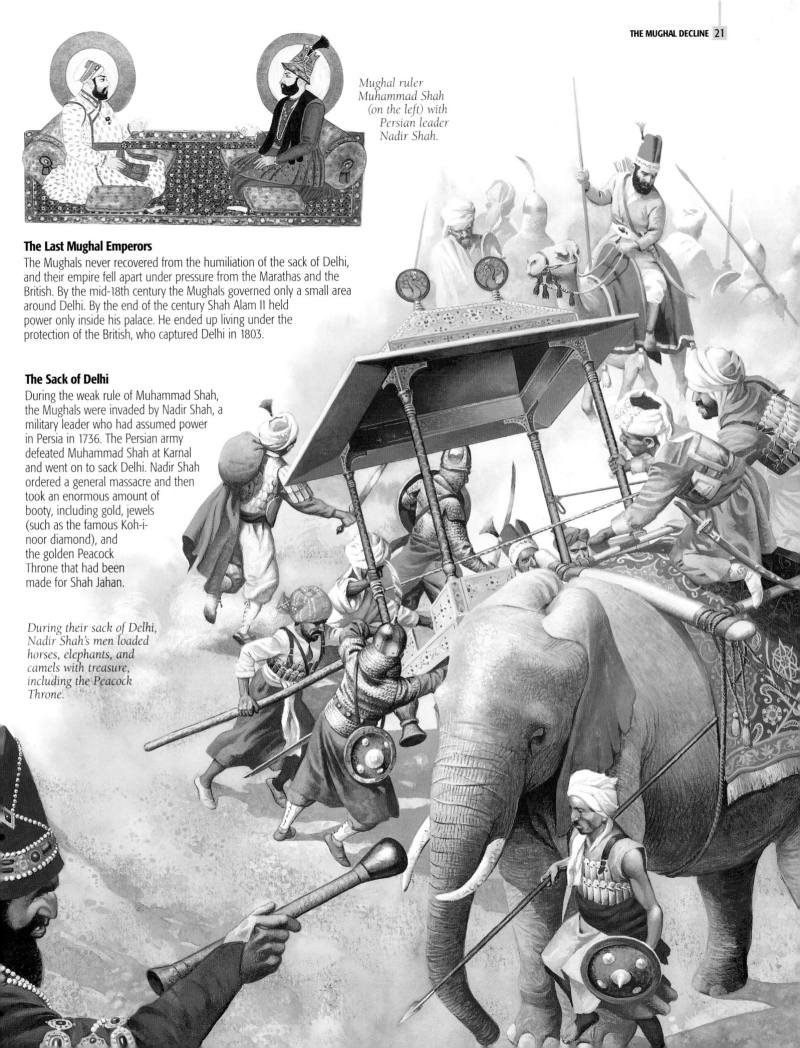

*Mughal ruler Muhammad Shah (on the left) with Persian leader Nadir Shah.*

## The Last Mughal Emperors

The Mughals never recovered from the humiliation of the sack of Delhi, and their empire fell apart under pressure from the Marathas and the British. By the mid-18th century the Mughals governed only a small area around Delhi. By the end of the century Shah Alam II held power only inside his palace. He ended up living under the protection of the British, who captured Delhi in 1803.

## The Sack of Delhi

During the weak rule of Muhammad Shah, the Mughals were invaded by Nadir Shah, a military leader who had assumed power in Persia in 1736. The Persian army defeated Muhammad Shah at Karnal and went on to sack Delhi. Nadir Shah ordered a general massacre and then took an enormous amount of booty, including gold, jewels (such as the famous Koh-i-noor diamond), and the golden Peacock Throne that had been made for Shah Jahan.

*During their sack of Delhi, Nadir Shah's men loaded horses, elephants, and camels with treasure, including the Peacock Throne.*

# Dynasties and Kingdoms of India

Before the arrival of the Mughals, several great dynasties ruled the sultanate of Delhi. There were kingdoms and empires in other parts of the subcontinent, some Muslim and others Hindu. There was constant conflict between different peoples and regions. When Afghan invaders finally defeated the Marathas in the 18th century, the Sikhs were able to establish themselves as rulers of the Punjab region. By that time the British East India Company controlled Bengal and had a strong foothold in the subcontinent.

*This painting from Rajasthan of the Hindu goddess Radha dates from about 1760.*

### Mughal conflict

From early in the 16th century, independent Muslim sultanates and Hindu kingdoms came into conflict with the growing Mughal empire. As the Mughals expanded their influence, they fought and conquered others, advancing into the Deccan at the beginning of the 17th century. The Mughals conquered Ahmadnagar in 1636, and 50 years later went on to capture the powerful kingdom of Bijapur.

*Gol Gumbaz, the domed tomb of Muhammad Adil Shah (ruled 1626–56) in Bijapur.*

### Rajput Painting

The Rajputs of the northwestern region developed their own style of art in the 16th and early 17th centuries. Rajput rulers were great art patrons, and their preferred style was traditional and romantic. Favorite subjects were the great Hindu god Krishna and his companion Radha. Many paintings were kept in boxes or albums, which were passed around for viewing.

### Maratha Empire

The Marathas founded their Hindu empire in western India (in the present-day state of Maharashtra) in 1674, when Shivaji united warrior chiefs into a federation. They increased their empire by conquest, fighting the Mughals for territory during the reign of Aurangzeb (see page 20). But the Marathas failed to take Delhi, and in 1761 were defeated by an invading Afghan army. This caused the decline of their empire.

*Maratha founder Shivali, who was known as a tough warrior and a tolerant ruler.*

*Bijapur ruler Ali Adil Shah II (reigned 1657–72) is fanned by a servant.*

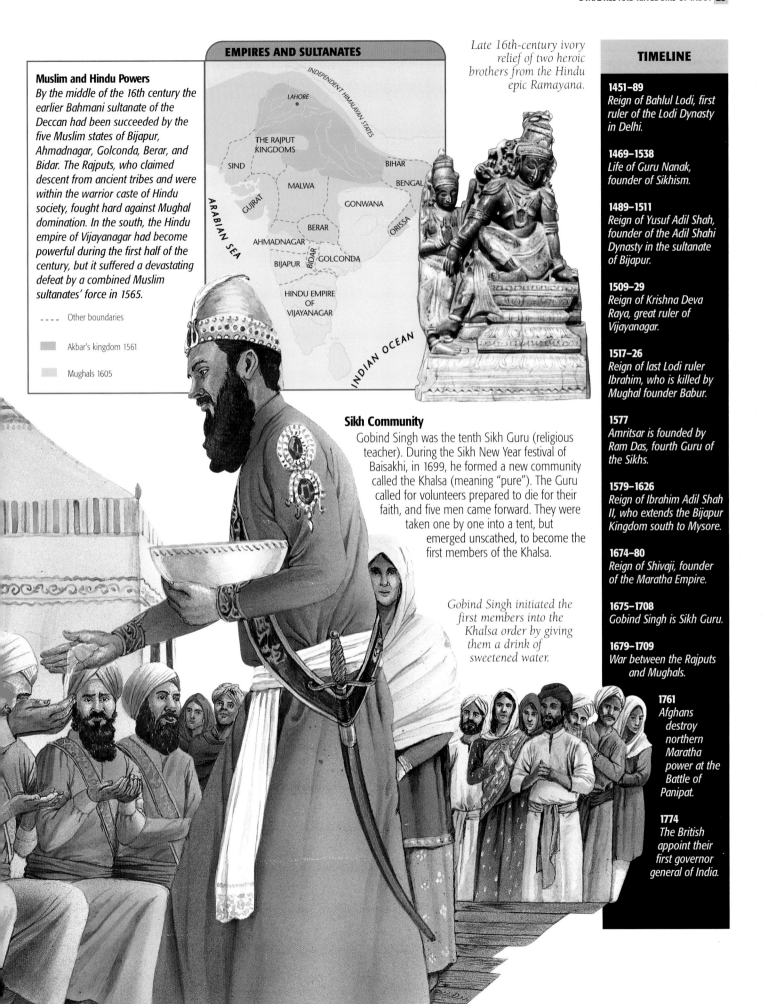

## Muslim and Hindu Powers

*By the middle of the 16th century the earlier Bahmani sultanate of the Deccan had been succeeded by the five Muslim states of Bijapur, Ahmadnagar, Golconda, Berar, and Bidar. The Rajputs, who claimed descent from ancient tribes and were within the warrior caste of Hindu society, fought hard against Mughal domination. In the south, the Hindu empire of Vijayanagar had become powerful during the first half of the century, but it suffered a devastating defeat by a combined Muslim sultanates' force in 1565.*

**EMPIRES AND SULTANATES**

- - - -  Other boundaries

▨  Akbar's kingdom 1561

▨  Mughals 1605

*Late 16th-century ivory relief of two heroic brothers from the Hindu epic Ramayana.*

## Sikh Community

Gobind Singh was the tenth Sikh Guru (religious teacher). During the Sikh New Year festival of Baisakhi, in 1699, he formed a new community called the Khalsa (meaning "pure"). The Guru called for volunteers prepared to die for their faith, and five men came forward. They were taken one by one into a tent, but emerged unscathed, to become the first members of the Khalsa.

*Gobind Singh initiated the first members into the Khalsa order by giving them a drink of sweetened water.*

## TIMELINE

**1451–89**
*Reign of Bahlul Lodi, first ruler of the Lodi Dynasty in Delhi.*

**1469–1538**
*Life of Guru Nanak, founder of Sikhism.*

**1489–1511**
*Reign of Yusuf Adil Shah, founder of the Adil Shahi Dynasty in the sultanate of Bijapur.*

**1509–29**
*Reign of Krishna Deva Raya, great ruler of Vijayanagar.*

**1517–26**
*Reign of last Lodi ruler Ibrahim, who is killed by Mughal founder Babur.*

**1577**
*Amritsar is founded by Ram Das, fourth Guru of the Sikhs.*

**1579–1626**
*Reign of Ibrahim Adil Shah II, who extends the Bijapur Kingdom south to Mysore.*

**1674–80**
*Reign of Shivaji, founder of the Maratha Empire.*

**1675–1708**
*Gobind Singh is Sikh Guru.*

**1679–1709**
*War between the Rajputs and Mughals.*

**1761**
*Afghans destroy northern Maratha power at the Battle of Panipat.*

**1774**
*The British appoint their first governor general of India.*

# Islamic Arts

The Ottoman, Safavid, and Mughal empires shared a common Islamic tradition in art and architecture. Though the empires developed their own distinctive styles, individual artists and architects moved between the territories, exchanging ideas and styles as well as specific works of art. The great mosques of Istanbul and Isfahan defined the architecture of the Ottomans and Safavids, while the Mughal emperors became known for their monumental tombs and palaces. In the visual arts, the Islamic tradition emphasized the use of geometric and floral designs throughout the empires.

*This late 16th-century Ottoman prayer rug features a mihrab (prayer niche in a mosque). The rug is woven in wool, silk, and cotton.*

*This 16th-century silk caftan has a typical floral design that includes the most popular flowers—tulips.*

*This Mughal craftsman is shown preparing paper for the court painters.*

## Textiles

From the 16th century, Ottoman carpets followed earlier Persian designs. Many of the woven designs were based on existing textiles, and silk was used for more valuable carpets, along with wool and cotton. The Ottoman region was an important link in the silk trade from China, and the commercial production of textiles expanded as exports to Europe increased.

## Decoration

From the earliest times Islamic architects and designers used richly colored tiles to decorate the walls of mosques and other important buildings. The glazed ceramic tiles were arranged as a mosaic in wonderful geometric patterns. Later, use was made of glazed bricks and larger square tiles. Monumental inscriptions were often included in the tiled decoration.

## Court Painters

Many of the Mughal emperors were great patrons of the arts, and painting became a favored art at court. At first painters worked mainly on book illustrations and miniatures, using Persian and Indian history and literature as sources, as well as making portraits of the emperor and his family. Some Mughal painting involved a team of artists, with one composing the picture, another adding color, and a third concentrating on individual figures.

*One of the minarets that stand at the Imam Mosque beside the public square at Isfahan. The mosque was built in 1612–30.*

*The façade of the Tilla Kari (or "gold-covered") madrasa and mosque, at Registan Square in Samarkand, is decorated with glazed bricks and tiled panels.*

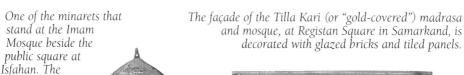

## Mughal Architecture

The Mughal emperors gave great importance to architecture as a symbol of power and authority. They introduced Indian themes to the Islamic tradition of decoration, and became highly skilled in the artistic use of red sandstone and white marble. Mughal architects used these materials to build and decorate wonderful forts, palaces, and tombs. One of the most famous sandstone buildings is the Red Fort at Delhi (built 1639–48). The most famous building of all is the Taj Mahal at Agra (1632–43). Both were built for Shah Jahan.

*The main structure of the Taj Mahal mausoleum, including the dome, is built of brick faced with white marble. Other buildings within the complex are built of sandstone.*

*Parts of the Red Fort were decorated with floral designs of inlaid semi-precious stones.*

# The Early Ming Dynasty

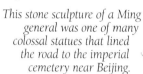

The first emperor of the Chinese dynasty that took over from the Mongols in the 14th century chose the dynastic name Ming, meaning "brilliant." The new ruler set out to wipe out the memory of foreign occupation and restore the empire's past greatness. This was largely achieved by successive Ming emperors, who were to go on to rule China for nearly 300 years. Their capital moved from Nanjing to Beijing, where the imperial court was housed in a rectangular city within the city.

*Portrait of Emperor Hongwu (reigned 1368–98), who was a harsh ruler and famously ugly.*

*This stone sculpture of a Ming general was one of many colossal statues that lined the road to the imperial cemetery near Beijing.*

## Founding the Dynasty

The Mongols had ruled China for 89 years when their Yuan Dynasty came to an end. In 1368 rebel leader Zhu Yuanzhang, who controlled central and southern China, declared himself emperor (taking the title Hongwu, meaning "vast military power") and founded the Ming Dynasty. Hongwu captured Beijing, and by 1387 his troops had driven the Mongols out of the provinces.

*This watchtower, now restored, was built during the Ming period as part of the extended Great Wall.*

## The Third Emperor

Hongwu was succeeded by his young grandson, who ruled as Jianwen (1399–1402). During the reign of Yongle, the fourth son of Hongwu, Beijing was completely rebuilt –including the construction of the Forbidden City–and became the official capital. Yongle had a good military and scholarly education, and he was a strong ruler.

## Mongol Threat

The Mongols remained a threat to the Ming Empire. Yongle himself led five campaigns against them, and he died during the last of these. The Ming emperors strengthened existing parts of the Great Wall and added new sections to protect their northern borders against invaders. They built extra walls at passes and in valleys, adding large watchtowers and beacon towers.

## TIMELINE

**1368**
Zhu Yuanzhang (1328–98) founds the Ming Dynasty as Emperor Hongwu.

**1380**
Hongwu has his prime minister executed for plotting against him; the emperor later abolishes the post altogether.

**1403–24**
Reign of Yongle.

**1405–33**
Naval commander Zheng He leads seven voyages from eastern China to the Indian Ocean.

**1406–21**
Building of the Forbidden City.

**1417**
Confucian text The Great Compendium of the Philosophy of Human Nature is published.

**1421**
The capital moves from Nanjing to Beijing.

**1426–35**
Reign of Xuande, a great patron of the arts at the imperial court.

**1436–49, 1457–64**
The interrupted reigns of Emperor Zhengtong/ Tianshun.

*This painting of the Sun was made in 1425 by Emperor Hongxi, who took an interest in astronomy.*

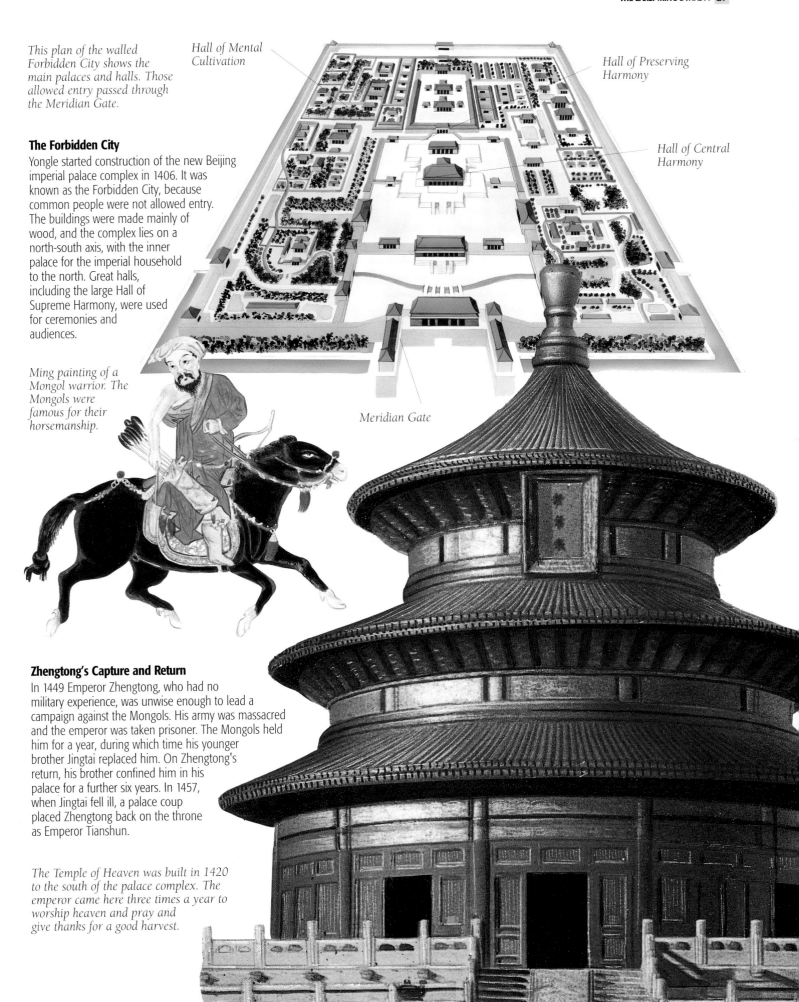

*This plan of the walled Forbidden City shows the main palaces and halls. Those allowed entry passed through the Meridian Gate.*

Hall of Mental Cultivation

Hall of Preserving Harmony

Hall of Central Harmony

## The Forbidden City

Yongle started construction of the new Beijing imperial palace complex in 1406. It was known as the Forbidden City, because common people were not allowed entry. The buildings were made mainly of wood, and the complex lies on a north-south axis, with the inner palace for the imperial household to the north. Great halls, including the large Hall of Supreme Harmony, were used for ceremonies and audiences.

*Ming painting of a Mongol warrior. The Mongols were famous for their horsemanship.*

Meridian Gate

## Zhengtong's Capture and Return

In 1449 Emperor Zhengtong, who had no military experience, was unwise enough to lead a campaign against the Mongols. His army was massacred and the emperor was taken prisoner. The Mongols held him for a year, during which time his younger brother Jingtai replaced him. On Zhengtong's return, his brother confined him in his palace for a further six years. In 1457, when Jingtai fell ill, a palace coup placed Zhengtong back on the throne as Emperor Tianshun.

*The Temple of Heaven was built in 1420 to the south of the palace complex. The emperor came here three times a year to worship heaven and pray and give thanks for a good harvest.*

# The Ming Empire

Despite increasing trade and an expanding economy, the Ming emperors and their imperial government gradually became weaker. Threats from the north remained, and though there was more contact with the rest of the world through trade, the emperors generally remained conservative and inward-looking. High taxes caused unrest, and famine and drought led to open revolt. This eventually caused the downfall of the dynasty, as rebels within the empire opened the way for Manchus from the north to take over.

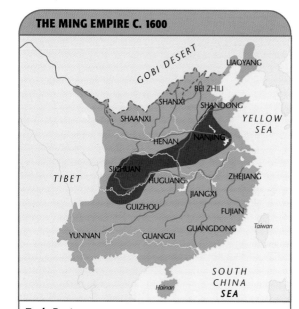

**THE MING EMPIRE C. 1600**

GOBI DESERT
LIAOYANG
SHANXI
BEI ZHILI
SHANDONG
SHAANXI
YELLOW SEA
HENAN
NANJING
TIBET
SICHUAN
ZHEJIANG
HUGUANG
JIANGXI
GUIZHOU
FUJIAN
YUNNAN
GUANGDONG
Taiwan
GUANGXI
SOUTH CHINA SEA
Hainan

**Trade Routes**
*During the 16th century maritime trade became more important and ports grew. Ningbo gave access to and from Japan, Quanzhou to Taiwan, and Guangzhou to Southeast Asia. Cotton textiles, silk, porcelain, and tea were the main exports, and American silver was imported via Manila. In 1557 the Portuguese were allowed to establish a permanent trading base at Macao. But relations between the Chinese and European merchants were not always good.*

Ming territory c. 1590 — — — Great Wall

Popular uprising 1636-41 ——— Chinese trade routes under the Ming Empire

## Philosophy and Religion

During the early Ming period, leading figures in the empire followed the interpretation of Confucianism that had been made by the 12th-century philosopher Zhu Xi. Emperor Hongzhi (reigned 1488–1505), for example, received a strict Confucian education. By this time Buddhism and Taoism were less influential, though Emperor Jiajing (reigned 1522–67) was a Taoist who tried to suppress Buddhism. His son and successor Longqing expelled the Taoists from the imperial court.

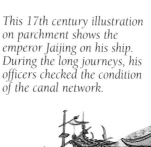

*Late Ming bronze statuette of the Taoist god of riches. Taoism was influenced by Chinese folk religion.*

*This 17th century illustration on parchment shows the emperor Jaijing on his ship. During the long journeys, his officers checked the condition of the canal network.*

## Rebellion

Severe famine in 1628 led to despair. Army deserters and laid-off soldiers formed bandit gangs, and others rebelled against imperial rule. Tax increases in 1639, followed by floods, made the situation worse. Workers rioted and tenants rose up against their landlords. One rebel leader, Li Zicheng, finally captured the capital and Emperor Chongzheng committed suicide. This was the perfect opportunity for the Manchus, who drove the rebels out and seized power.

*Peasants rebelled against landowners. In this scene, former servants loot an estate. The landowner can do nothing as his wife is forced to serve the rebels.*

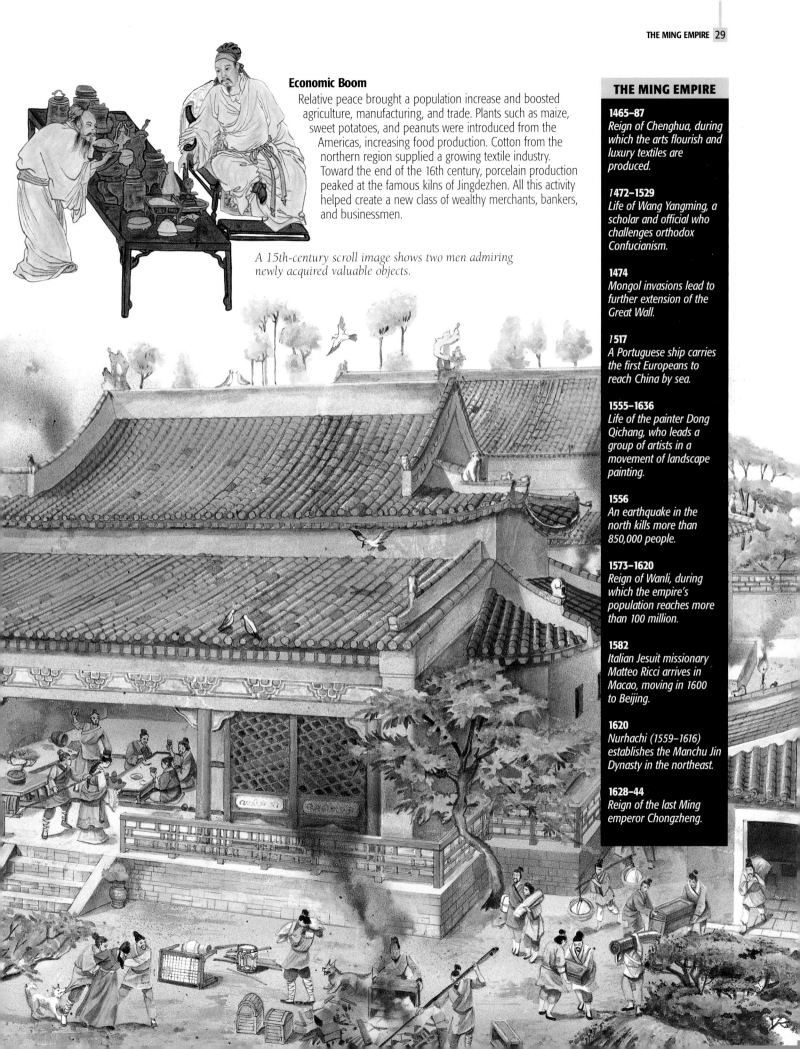

## Economic Boom

Relative peace brought a population increase and boosted agriculture, manufacturing, and trade. Plants such as maize, sweet potatoes, and peanuts were introduced from the Americas, increasing food production. Cotton from the northern region supplied a growing textile industry. Toward the end of the 16th century, porcelain production peaked at the famous kilns of Jingdezhen. All this activity helped create a new class of wealthy merchants, bankers, and businessmen.

*A 15th-century scroll image shows two men admiring newly acquired valuable objects.*

## THE MING EMPIRE

**1465–87**
*Reign of Chenghua, during which the arts flourish and luxury textiles are produced.*

**1472–1529**
*Life of Wang Yangming, a scholar and official who challenges orthodox Confucianism.*

**1474**
*Mongol invasions lead to further extension of the Great Wall.*

**1517**
*A Portuguese ship carries the first Europeans to reach China by sea.*

**1555–1636**
*Life of the painter Dong Qichang, who leads a group of artists in a movement of landscape painting.*

**1556**
*An earthquake in the north kills more than 850,000 people.*

**1573–1620**
*Reign of Wanli, during which the empire's population reaches more than 100 million.*

**1582**
*Italian Jesuit missionary Matteo Ricci arrives in Macao, moving in 1600 to Beijing.*

**1620**
*Nurhachi (1559–1616) establishes the Manchu Jin Dynasty in the northeast.*

**1628–44**
*Reign of the last Ming emperor Chongzheng.*

# The Early Qing Dynasty

The Manchus were quick to seize their opportunity to capture Beijing, take over from the Ming Dynasty, and expand their northern territory into a vast empire. During the 17th and 18th centuries, they were able to extend Qing control even further. The Manchus made up a small percentage of their new empire's population, and there was some resistance to their customs. The Qing emperors adopted many of the Ming forms of government and administration, but they kept their own military system based on separate "banner" units.

*Painting from 1760 of one of the emperor's warrior bodyguards.*

*A 17th-century statuette of a European.*

*This scroll painting by Giuseppe Castiglione shows Kazakh envoys presenting horses as tribute to Qianlong. It was painted in a style that combined Chinese and European techniques.*

*A Qing emperor's court boots.*

### The Manchus

The Manchus were descendants of the Jurchens from Manchuria (to the northeast of the Ming Empire). Their ancestors had ruled northern China in the 12th century, and in 1620 their chieftain Nurhachi started a new Manchu Dynasty. His son Huang Taiji (reigned 1626–43) ruled from their capital Shenyang and adopted the Chinese dynastic name Qing, meaning "pure." By 1644 Huang's six-year-old son Shunzhi ruled the new Qing Empire of China.

## Longest Reign

The second Qing emperor, Kangxi, succeeded his father at the age of eight and assumed full power six years later. His reign (1661–1722) was the longest in this or any other Chinese dynasty. As both a good administrator and military commander, Kangxi toured and inspected his vast empire. He also led the Qing army against the Mongols, who continued to threaten the Chinese borders. He had a great love of literature and was a patron of the arts.

*The young Kangxi at his studies. As emperor he set up studios for artists and architects in the Forbidden City.*

*This porcelain statuette of Guanyin, a Buddhist figure known in the West as the goddess of mercy, shows Western influences.*

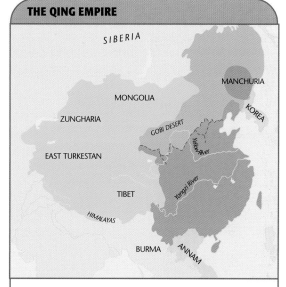

**THE QING EMPIRE**

SIBERIA

MANCHURIA

MONGOLIA

ZUNGHARIA

KOREA

EAST TURKESTAN

GOBI DESERT

Yellow River

TIBET

Yangzi River

HIMALAYAS

BURMA

ANNAM

## Qianlong's Empire

Kangxi's grandson Qianlong expanded the Qing Empire to its greatest extent. Success and wealth brought a further population boom, and farming production and manufacturing went up. Tea, cotton, and porcelain exports all increased. But rapid expansion also brought problems, and these were made worse in the emperor's later years by dependence on his corrupt minister Heshan.

### Expansion

*The Qing Empire expanded greatly in the 18th century, under Kangxi, Yongzheng, and Qianlong. A series of campaigns led to Tibet being brought under Chinese control, and in 1755–65 Qianlong's armies went west and swept through Central Asia. By then the empire covered present-day Mongolia and parts of Russia, and Chinese dominance was recognized in Korea, Vietnam, and Burma.*

- Additional area under Manchu Dynasty in 1760
- Manchu expansion by 1644
- Manchu homeland
- Manchu vassal state
- Area under Ming dynasty
- --- Great wall

## Jesuits at Court

Kangxi welcomed Jesuit missionaries at his court, admiring the Europeans' artistic and technical skills and appointing them as astronomers, cartographers, and physicians. Qianlong continued the tradition and even commissioned Jesuit architects to design his summer palace outside Beijing. The Jesuits were careful to blend their European ideas with Chinese styles.

# Japan in the Muromachi Period

In the early 14th century central military authority and government moved from Kamakura to Kyoto. A new family of shoguns came to power, and they continued to exercise authority over the imperial family. The period of rule by the Ashikaga shoguns (1338–1573) is called after its center of power, Muromachi. After a disastrous civil war in the 15th century, the shogunate lost authority and provincial warlords fought each other for land and power. This split Japan into hundreds of separate feudal states.

*Yoshimitsu had this Golden Pavilion built outside Kyoto in 1394.*

*Takauji was a powerful warrior as well as a skilled statesman.*

## The Muromachi Shogunate

Takauji's grandson Yoshimitsu (1358–1408) moved his headquarters to the Muromachi district of Kyoto, giving the shogunate its name. Yoshimitsu was a powerful shogun, who brought the two rival imperial courts together again. Nevertheless, during his rule provincial military governors gained more influence, raising taxes from local landowners.

## The Ashikaga Family

The Ashikaga family had become one of the most powerful in Japan during the 13th-century Kamakura period. Having driven the emperor from Kyoto, Ashikaga Takauji (1305–58) had himself appointed shogun by a rival emperor in 1338. This marked the beginning of the Ashikaga shogunate. Takauji was a cultured man who wrote poetry and helped the development of Zen Buddhism.

## Increasing Trade

Yoshimitsu stopped southern feudal lords from raiding the Chinese coast and set up formal trade with Ming-dynasty China and Korea. He even adopted the title "King of Japan" in his dealings with the Ming government. Increased trade at home and abroad helped create a new class of Japanese merchants, as farming, commerce, and mining all grew and improved.

## Onin War

Civil war broke out in 1467 between rival regional warlords. They took the opportunity to take sides in a dispute over the succession to the shogunate. Yoshimasa had made his younger brother his heir, but then the shogun's wife gave birth to a son. Full-scale war broke out around Kyoto and lasted for ten years. The shogun abdicated in favor of his son, but the shogunate was greatly weakened.

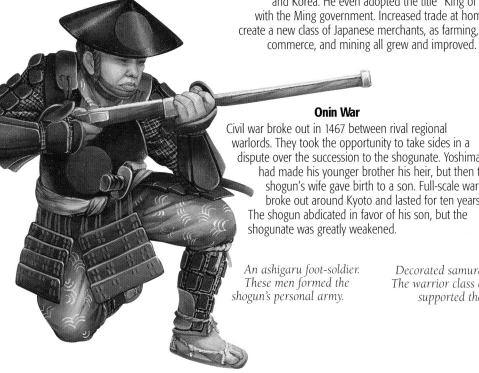

*An ashigaru foot-soldier. These men formed the shogun's personal army.*

*Decorated samurai swords. The warrior class of samurai supported the provincial feudal lords.*

**TIMELINE**

**1336**
*Ashikaga Takauji's rebel forces drive Emperor Go-Daigo (reigned 1318–39) from Kyoto to Yoshino; there are two rival imperial courts until 1392.*

**1363–1443**
*Life of Zeami Motokiyo, a great playwright of No theater under the patronage of Yoshimitsu. 1368–94 Ashikaga Yoshimitsu rules as shogun, moving his administration to Muromachi in 1378.*

**1449–73**
*Ashikaga Yoshimasa rules as shogun.*

**1483**
*Yoshimasa builds the Silver Pavilion as his retirement retreat in the Eastern Hills of Kyoto.*

**1488**
*A Poem of One Hundred Links is composed by three poets, Sogi (1421–1502), Shohaku (1443–1527), and Socho (1448–1532).*

**1543**
*Portuguese sailors in a Chinese boat become the first Europeans to visit Japan.*

**1549**
*Spanish Jesuit missionary Francis Xavier (1506–52) arrives in Japan.*

**1573**
*Yoshiaki is deposed as the last Ashikaga shogun.*

## Cultural Developments

There was a flowering of Japanese culture in the 14th century. Masked No theater followed on from ancient forms of dance drama and festival rituals. A form of "linked verse" developed, in which three or more poets supplied alternating verses. Zen Buddhists encouraged these arts, as well as those of ink painting, flower arrangement, and the tea ceremony.

*A No mask. All the actors were male, but they sometimes wore female masks.*

*The ritual of the tea ceremony was a study in refinement and elegance.*

*No dramas were popular with the nobility. A performance was usually made up of five serious, stylized plays separated by comic interludes.*

## The Oda Regime

Born into a noble family, Oda Nobunaga (1534–82) was a powerful, ambitious warrior. Originally a supporter of the shogun Ashikaga Yoshiaki, Nobunaga turned against him and finally deposed him in 1573. After occupying Kyoto, Nobunaga built Azuchi Castle, selected able generals, and fought his way to domination over central Japan.

### TIMELINE

**1582**
*Having been wounded by a rebel in an attempted coup, Oda Nobunaga commits suicide.*

**1585–98**
*Toyotomi Hideyoshi is chief imperial minister.*

**1592–98**
*Toyotomi Hideyoshi's armies invade Korea twice, but withdraw after his death.*

**1600**
*Tokugawa Ieyasu defeats his rivals at the Battle of Sekigahara.*

**1615**
*The shogunate issues the first of a series of codes of conduct based on Confucian principles.*

**1637–41**
*Expulsion of Portuguese traders.*

**1638**
*Up to 37,000 Japanese Christians are massacred at Hara castle.*

**1703**
*Edo is almost destroyed by an earthquake and fire.*

**1725–70**
*Life of artist Suzuki Harunobu, famous for his graceful paintings and wood-block prints.*

**1760**
*Peasant uprisings break out.*

# The Unification of Japan

From 1574 great efforts were made to reunify the warring regions of Japan. The years 1574 to 1600 are often called the Azuchi-Momoyama period. The name refers to castles built by the country's first great unifiers: Azuchi (beside Lake Biwa) was built by Oda Nobunaga, and Momoyama (in Kyoto) by his successor Toyotomi Hideyoshi. The third unifier, Tokugawa Ieyasu, moved his power base to Edo (modern Tokyo). In 1603 Ieyasu became shogun, founding the Tokugawa shogunate that was to rule unified Japan until 1867.

*Oda Nobunaga, who equipped many of his followers with muskets.*

## Society

In the 17th century Japanese society was governed by a strict system of military authority. Much of the power lay with the regional feudal lords, who in their own region made laws and collected taxes. The rest of society was divided into four classes: samurai warriors at the top, followed by farmers, artisans, and merchants. Despite their supposedly low status, many merchants came to enjoy great wealth.

*Painted wooden statuette of Zen Buddhist priest Ishin Suden (1569–1633), who helped draft new laws.*

## Ieyasu and Edo

Tokugawa Ieyasu (1542–1616) was a noble from eastern Japan, who became an ally of Hideyoshi and ruled as one of the regents for the shogun's heir. He controlled a large army, defeated his rivals in battle, and founded the Tokugawa shogunate. Ieyasu ran his government from Edo, which became the unified country's political center, though Kyoto remained the official capital throughout the Tokugawa period.

*A Christian is killed during the outbreak of violence in 1638.*

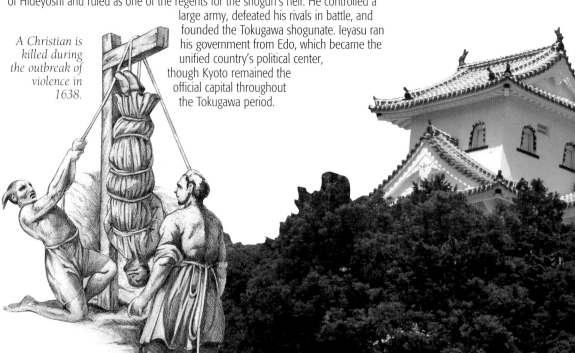

## HIDEYOSHI'S CONQUESTS

SEA OF JAPAN

HIROSAKI  HACHINOHE
AKITA  MORIOKA
HONJO
TSURUOKA  SHINJO
SENDAI
SHIBATA  YAMAGATA
NAGAOKA  YONEZAWA
IWAKI
TOYAMA  SHIRAKAWA
KANAZAWA  TAKASAKI  UTSONOMIYA
FUKUCHIYAMA  FUKUI  IIDA  Hojo
YONAGO  OBAMA  ODAWARA
MATSUE  KOBE  AZUCHI
HAMADA  HIMEJI  MOMOYAMA  NUMATSU
KITAKYUSHU  OSAKA  YOSHIDA
HAGI  HIROSHIMA  ISE
HAKATAKA  IMABARI  TANABE
NAGOYA  TOKUSHIMA
Chosokabe
HIRADO  FUNAI  UWAJIMA  MATSUYAMA
Shimazu  NOBEOKA
KAGOSHIMA  MIYAZAKI

PACIFIC OCEAN

### Toyotomi Hideyoshi

*Toyotomi Hideyoshi (1536–98) rose from humble peasant origins to become Oda Nobunaga's leading commander. After his leader's death, he won important battles against rivals, made good alliances, consolidated his power in Kyoto, and held control over most of Japan by 1590. The map shows the progression of the great commander's conquests.*

- Area conquered by Nobunaga and Hideyoshi by 1582
- Oda land
- Main *daimyo* house opposed to Hideyoshi, 1582
- Castle town
- → Toyotomi Hideyoshi's campaigns of unification
- — Area unified by Oda Nobunaga by 1582

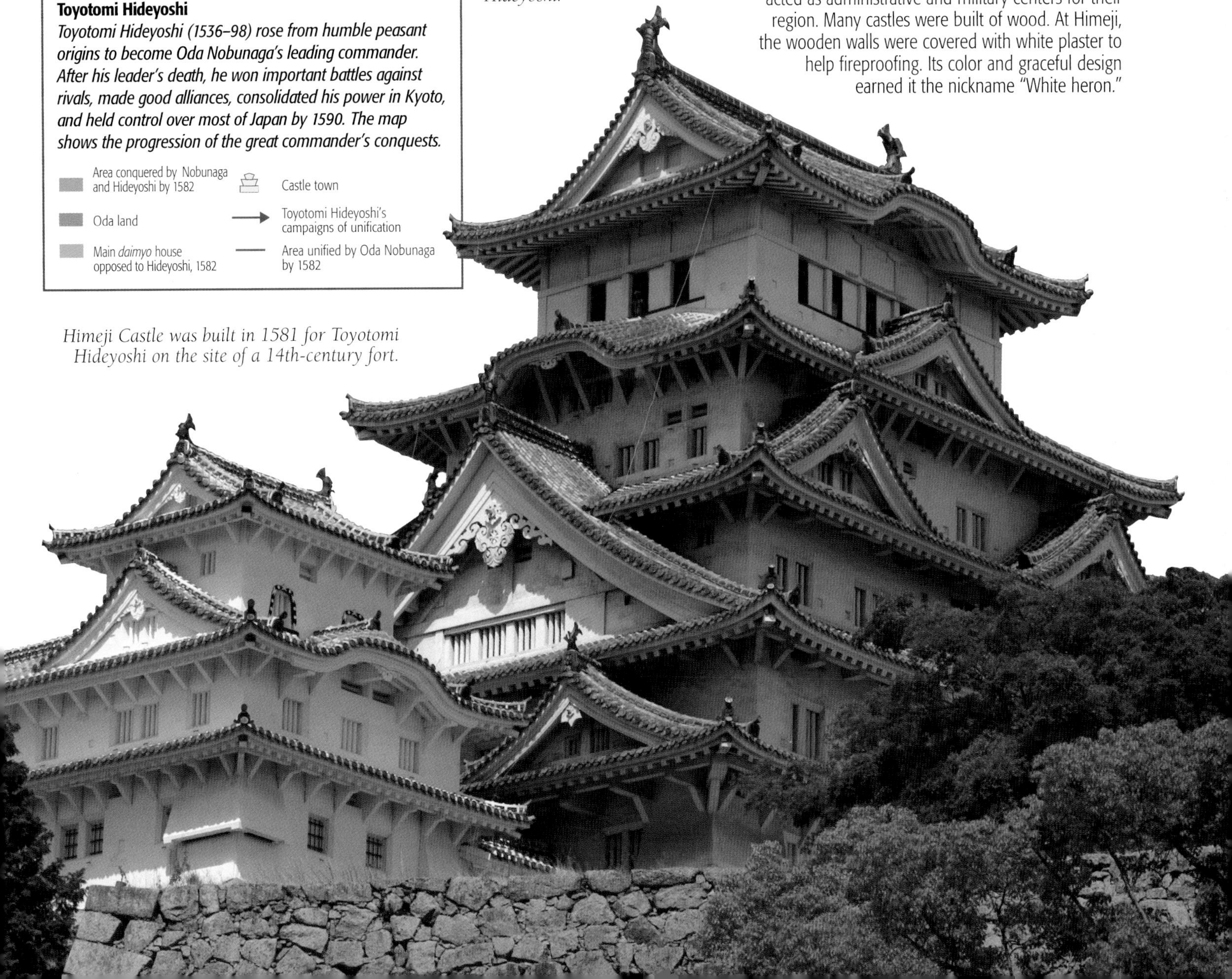

*Himeji Castle was built in 1581 for Toyotomi Hideyoshi on the site of a 14th-century fort.*

*A Japanese trading ship. Nagasaki became Japan's most important port for foreign trade in the late 16th century.*

*This lacquered wooden wine pot may have been used by Toyotomi Hideyoshi.*

### Castles

During the late 16th century regional warlords began building magnificent castles to protect themselves and their land. Towns grew around the castles and acted as administrative and military centers for their region. Many castles were built of wood. At Himeji, the wooden walls were covered with white plaster to help fireproofing. Its color and graceful design earned it the nickname "White heron."

*This Chosôn porcelain jar, with an iron brown glaze, is decorated with a dragon design.*

## Chosôn Society

The elite, scholarly class of Chosôn society was known as yangban, meaning "two groups" (referring to civilian and military officials). Members of this land-owning class were expected to cultivate the Confucian moral standards of others during the course of their duties. Many were accomplished artists. Beneath them in the hierarchy were craftsmen, peasants, and merchants. At the bottom of the social order were lowly butchers and gravediggers, as well as slaves.

*Painting from a late Chosôn Album of Scenes from Daily Life, which focused on people's everyday lives.*

### KOREA

**Japanese Invasion**
In 1592 Japan's ruler Toyotomi Hideyoshi (see page 35) sent a large army to invade Korea. With support from Ming China and great resistance by their navy, the Koreans forced the Japanese to withdraw. In 1597 the Japanese invaded again, but after Hideyoshi's death in the following year, they again withdrew. The map shows the regions where the Japanese campaigns took place and the area that they occupied.

- Area of Korea occupied by Japan 1593-98
- Main area of Korean resistance to Hideyoshi
- → Campaigns in Korea 1592
- → Korean and Ming Chinese counteroffensives
- → Toyotomi Hideyoshi's campaigns of unification

# Korea's Chosôn Dynasty

When a new dynasty came to power in Korea in 1392, its founder took up the ancient name of Chosôn for his kingdom. The dynasty of Yi rulers had close cultural ties with Ming China, to which it paid tribute. This was transferred to the Manchus (and their Chinese Qing Dynasty) after they ravaged the Chosôn capital Hanyang. The Chosôn rulers officially ended support for Buddhism and made theirs a united, Confucian state. Korean scholars made their own contribution to the theories of Confucianism.

## Yi's Turtle Ships

The Korean naval forces were led by Admiral Yi Sun-shin, who helped develop the famous kobukson, or "turtle ship" (named after its shape). This was the world's first ironclad warship, with armored plates to protect its crew. It was heavily armed, with a dragon's head at the bow through which cannons could be fired. Admiral Yi's efforts off the south coast left the Japanese army cut off, and his ships scored important victoriesduring both invasions.

*The ironclad "turtle's" upper deck was covered with spikes, to prevent enemies from boarding. It was powered by a combination of sails and oars.*

*Statue of Admiral Yi Sun-shin (1545–98), who became a Korean national hero.*

*The traditional wide-brimmed hat was seen as an expression of Confucian moderation.*

## THE CHOSÔN DYNASTY

**1392**
*General Yi Song-gye overthrows the last ruler of the Koryo Dynasty and founds the new dynasty, moving the capital to Hanyang (modern Seoul).*

**c.1400–50**
*Korean potters start to produce white porcelain.*

**1419–50**
*Reign of Sejong, when early Chosôn culture reaches its highest point.*

**1420**
*A royal academy is set up as a center of learning, allowing promising young scholars the opportunity to study.*

**1443**
*Development of the modern Korean alphabet, called Hangul, is completed.*

**1592–98**
*Two Japanese invasions fail, but leave much of Korea in ruins; scholars and craftworkers are taken away to Japan.*

**1627**
*Manchu nomads overrun northern Korea.*

**1681–1763**
*Life of Yi Ik, famous scholar of the silhak ("practical learning") movement, who deals with land reform and the abolition of slavery.*

**1724–76**
*Reign of Yongjo, during which the arts thrive.*

# Cambodia, Burma, and Thailand

From the beginning of the 15th to the end of the 18th century, the mainland region of Southeast Asia was made up of many small kingdoms. They vied with each other for power, and there was constant tension and conflict between Burma (or Myanmar), Siam (modern Thailand), and Cambodia. The many different peoples of the region had their own rich cultures, inherited from earlier empires. The region was never united, but it had one major religion across the kingdoms—Buddhism.

*This 15th-century glazed ceramic tile from Burma shows ass-headed demons from the army of the god of death. They tried in vain to prevent the Buddha from attaining enlightenment.*

*An 18th-century puppet of a Burmese king, from Rangoon.*

## Burma

The southern region of modern Burma (Myanmar) was dominated by the Mon people, until their kingdom fell to the Burmese Toungoo Dynasty in 1539. They made their capital at Pegu, which became a great center of Buddhism. The Mon rebelled in the mid-18th century, brought down the Toungoom, and captured the capital of Ava, another Burmese kingdom. A king named Alaungpaya (reigned 1752–60) reunified Burma, establishing a new dynasty and founding the city of Rangoon.

## Cambodia

The sacking and abandonment of its capital Angkor in 1431 marked the decline of the powerful Khmer Empire of Cambodia. The weakened Khmer court moved south to Lovek (near modern Phnom Penh), where a golden royal palace was built in 1553. During the 15th and 16th centuries the Khmer were almost constantly at war with the Siamese state of Ayutthaya, which further weakened the Cambodian state.

## Thailand

The Thai kingdom of Ayutthaya ruled the region around its capital of the same name from the mid-14th to mid-18th century. For much of that time the kingdom was at war with its neighbors, the Burmese and the Khmer. After the city of Ayutthaya was finally destroyed by the Burmese in 1767, a military commander took over, until a new dynasty of kings was founded 15 years later. The capital of the kingdom was Bangkok.

*In 1593 King Naresuan of Thailand (reigned 1590–1605) rode his war elephant against the crown prince of Burma during a Burmese invasion. The Thai king was victorious and became a national hero.*

## CAMBODIA, BURMA, AND THAILAND

MING EMPIRE

Andaman Sea

Gulf of Thailand

Strait of Malacca

SOUTH CHINA SEA

### A Diversity of Peoples

*The different peoples of the Burma–Thailand–Cambodia region were constantly in conflict with each other. Yet they were united by the religious tradition of Buddhism, following the ancient school of Theravada ("Doctrine of the Elders"). To the east of the region, the earlier Khmer Empire had followed Hindu-Buddhist traditions. Islam dominated Arakan to the northwest and Malaya to the south.*

Ayutthaya Kingdom (Siam), mid-15th century

Burmese Kingdom of Toungou at maximum extent, 1555

Burma, 1783

Khmers (Cambodia)

# Indonesia, Malaysia, Laos, and Vietnam

### Vietnam

The state of Dai Viet had been established in the 10th century. It was strongly influenced—and for some years controlled—by China. The Le Dynasty came to power in 1428, and later in the century conquered the Hindu kingdom of Champa to the south.

**B**y the time the Europeans arrived in the early 16th century, the mainland and islands of Southeast Asia were divided into many different kingdoms and sultanates. There was often conflict among them. This made things easier for the various East India Companies, which sent ships across the Indian Ocean in search of precious goods, especially spices. The route to the Spice Islands led through the strategically important Strait of Malacca, between the Malay Peninsula and Sumatra (in modern Indonesia).

*Painted stone sculpture of a spiritual guardian. It comes from the Thien Mu Buddhist pagoda, first built in Hue, Vietnam, in 1601.*

*Map of the port of Malacca, which controlled the strait linking the Indian Ocean with the South China Sea.*

*Hat Makmo ("melon stupa"), a Buddhist temple built in 1504 by the consort of Laotian king Visunarat (reigned 1500–20).*

### The Malay State

During the 15th century the Muslim port of Malacca became an important trading center. It was a vital capture for the Portuguese in 1511 and the Dutch 130 years later. The Malays established other kingdoms on the peninsula, including Johore. In the 18th century the Buginese from Sulawesi invaded, captured Johore, and established further sultanates. The British arrived towards the end of the century.

### Laos

The unified Laotian kingdom of Lan Xang was established in the mid-14th century with Khmer help. Theravada Buddhism was introduced during the reign of the founder Fa Ngum (reigned 1353–74). Except for a period of rule by the Burmese, the kingdom lasted continuously until 1713, when it split into three separate kingdoms—Vien Chan (around the present capital of Laos, Vientiane), Champassak, and Luang Prabang. These kingdoms came under Thai control during the 18th century.

**c.1403**
*A Sumatran prince sets up the sultanate of Malacca on the Malaysian coast.*

**1488–1511**
*Reign of Mahmud Shah as sultan of Malacca; after the Portuguese invasion, he founds the kingdom of Johore.*

**1574–1637**
*Laos is ruled by Burma (Myanmar)*

**1600–64**
*East India Companies are formed: British (1600), Dutch (1602), Danish (1616), and French (1664).*

**1641**
*The Dutch seize Malacca from the Portuguese.*

**1677**
*The ruler of the Javanese kingdom of Mataram asks the Dutch to help fight rebels and gives trading rights in return.*

**1705–48**
*Life of the celebrated Vietnamese poet Doan Thi Diem.*

**1786**
*The British East India Company sets up a trading base on the Malayan island of Penang.*

**1778**
*Vientiane comes under Siamese (Thai) control.*

**1802**
*Gia Long becomes emperor of Dai Viet, which he renames Vietnam.*

A traditional wooden and leather puppet used in Javanese shadow plays of Hindu epics.

### European Presence

*After the Portuguese arrived in Malaysia early in the 16th century, European explorers, traders, and settlers made a great impact on the Indonesian islands. Followed by the Dutch and British, the Portuguese opened up the sea route from Europe to the Spice Islands (the Maluku province of Indonesia, or the Moluccas). The map shows the territories controlled by European nations by the 18th century.*

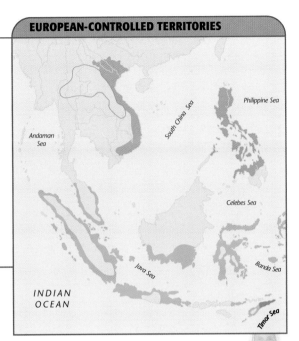

**EUROPEAN-CONTROLLED TERRITORIES**

- Empire of Annam, 1783
- Spanish territory, 1783
- Lao Kingdom of Lan Chang at maximum extent, 1548
- Dutch territory, 1783
- Portuguese territory, 1783

Andaman Sea

South China Sea

Philippine Sea

Celebes Sea

Java Sea

Banda Sea

INDIAN OCEAN

Timor Sea

### Indonesia

The Hindu Majapahit kingdom of Java dominated the region of present-day Indonesia until the late 15th century. By that time Islam had spread through the islands, and new Muslim trading kingdoms vied with each other for supremacy. In the following century the Portuguese established trading posts, and the first Dutch fleet arrived in 1596, landing at Bantam on the coast of Java. The Dutch East India Company ensured that their nation became the dominant power in Indonesia.

*Pilgrims visit the Javanese tomb of Maulana Malik Ibrahim, who died in 1419. He was one of the Wali Sanga ("nine saints of Islam"), who brought Islam to Java.*

# Art and Culture in East Asia

Chinese cultural styles and artistic techniques made their impression throughout East Asia. The Chinese love of calligraphy and skill in producing decorated pottery, and especially delicate porcelain, influenced the artists and art-lovers of Korea and Japan. Throughout the region rulers and their governments promoted excellence among their artists, setting up official academies and workshops and acting as patrons for painters and poets. Many results of their work can still be seen today.

### Literature

In China, Ming emperors restored competitive literary examinations and scholarly works were held in great respect. The educated elite disliked the colloquial literature that became more popular by the 16th century. Japanese adoption of printing in the 17th century also encouraged popular literature, since the classics existed only as manuscripts. In Korea, the Hangul alphabet developed in the 15th century was used for more popular works, but scholars continued to write in classical Chinese.

*Illustration for* Dream of Red Mansions, *a 120-chapter Chinese novel written by Cao Zhan (1715–64), famous for its sensitive portrayal of female characters.*

*This poem was written in the new Korean alphabet by Emperor Sejong (reigned 1419–50).*

### Painting

Ming-dynasty imperial patronage ensured that painters were highly regarded. Their style gradually became less academic as paintings showed more self-expression, especially in landscapes. Chinese painters influenced Korean artists, who also chose to show more realistic scenes of daily life. In Japan, the famous Kano school of painters reflected the official Confucian view of a well-ordered society, while other painters were more individualistic.

*A 17th-century Japanese screen painting of the wind god.*

### Science and Medicine

The 16th-century Chinese scholar Li Shizhen compiled a comprehensive compendium of more than 8,000 herbal remedies, following ancient prescriptions. Chinese physicians understood blood circulation, using acupuncture to ensure a good flow of chi, or "life force." Many scientific books were taken from China to Korea and Japan, including works on mathematics. By the 17th century Japan was also influenced by European medicine introduced by Jesuit missionaries and Dutch physicians.

*This Chinese ivory figure from the Ming period was used to teach female anatomy to medical students.*

*This 18th-century Korean screen painting of a bookshelf shows a Confucian respect for learning.*

## The Nine Dragon Screen

Emperor Qianlong (reigned 1736–95) refurbished and extended the Forbidden City in Beijing (see page 27). One of his additions was a screen wall covered with glazed tiles, which was completed in 1771 to protect the northeast section of the City. Nine writhing dragons appear on the screen in ceramic relief, representing in the highest single number the principle of heaven and the emperor as the son of heaven.

## Ceramics

The Chinese ceramics industry flourished during the Ming period, producing porcelain and other wares of exceptional quality. Porcelain production reached its peak at the Jingdezhen imperial kilns in the first half of the 18th century. In Korea, the Chosôn government also supported an official kiln to produce blue-and-white porcelain, but standards never reached the heights of Ming ware. In the 17th century, skilled Japanese potters specialized in vessels for the tea ceremony.

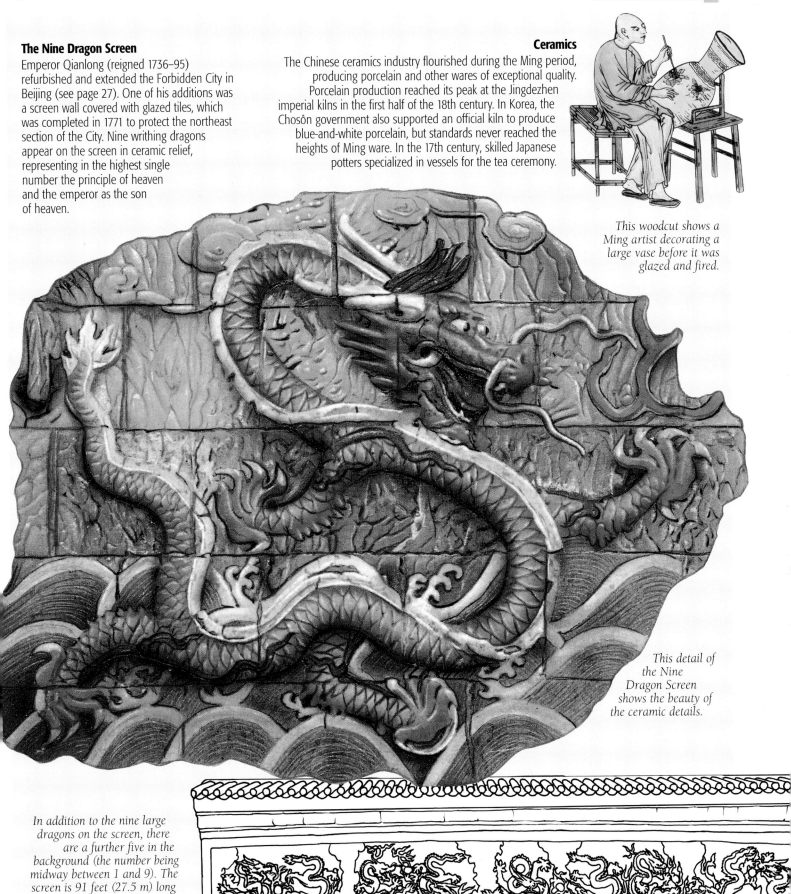

*This woodcut shows a Ming artist decorating a large vase before it was glazed and fired.*

*This detail of the Nine Dragon Screen shows the beauty of the ceramic details.*

*In addition to the nine large dragons on the screen, there are a further five in the background (the number being midway between 1 and 9). The screen is 91 feet (27.5 m) long and is covered with 270 tiles.*

This mechanical toy of a tiger attacking a British soldier belonged to Tipu Sultan, ruler of Mysore.

# The European Impact

The Europeans fought with each other, as well as with native populations, for dominance of Africa and Asia. In Africa, explorers and invaders concentrated on the Guinea coast, where they found plenty to interest them, including ivory, gold, and slaves. The Portuguese and then the Dutch dominated Southeast Asia and the spice trade. The British concentrated on India, where they quickly became involved in war and politics to protect their trade.

King Alkemy of Guinea, who traded slaves with the Europeans.

## Africa

The Portuguese began trading on the West African coast in the late 15th century, leading the way for others. They found many attractive goods in forested lands around the Gulf of Guinea, dividing them into regions according to the resources they offered. The Pepper or Grain Coast (in present-day Liberia) offered a spice called grains of paradise; then came the Ivory Coast, Gold Coast (Ghana), and Slave Coast (Togo, Benin, and Nigeria).

Portrait of the Scottish explorer Mungo Park (1771–1806), who made two expeditions along the Niger River in West Africa.

## Southeast Asia

The Spanish founded Manila in 1571, and by the end of the 16th century most of the islands of the Philippines (named after Phillip II of Spain) were under their control. There was opposition from the Portuguese, and then from the Dutch, who were expanding their East Indies empire. The Spanish also had to deal with frequent uprisings by the native population and with attacks by Muslim pirates.

Detail of an 18th-century Siamese lacquer panel, showing a Dutch merchant as an enemy of the Buddha.

Spanish Catholics founded the University of Santo Tomas in Manila in 1611. The city became the centre of Roman Catholicism in Southeast Asia.

## Far East

The early Ming emperors discouraged European traders from visiting China, considering them to be pirates and smugglers. By the end of the 16th century they were more tolerant, and in 1600 the Jesuit missionary Matteo Ricci arrived in Beijing. This was 51 years after Francis Xavier had first visited Japan. In the following century, European traders were expelled from Japan and Japanese Christians were massacred.

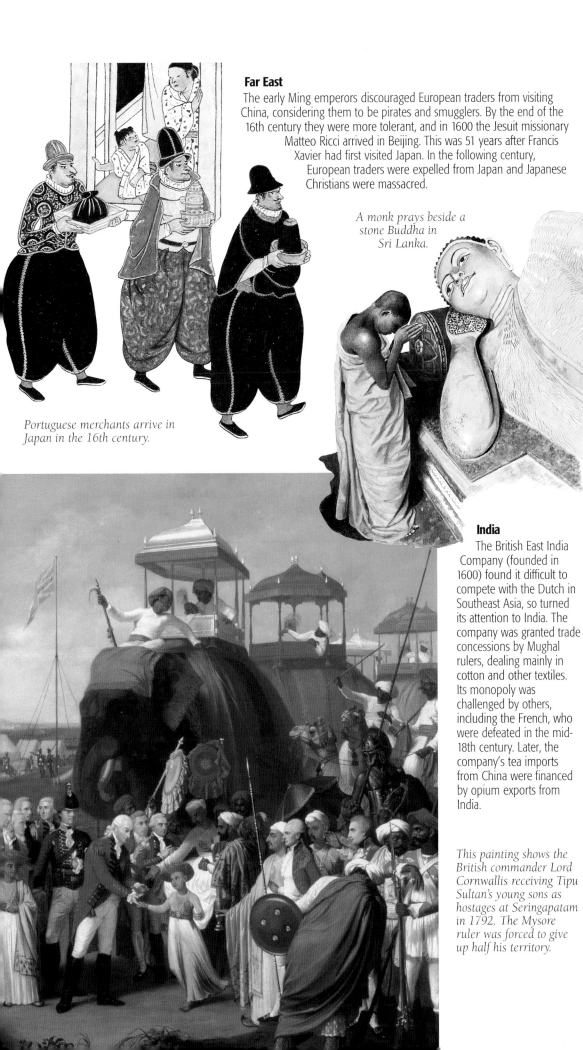

*Portuguese merchants arrive in Japan in the 16th century.*

*A monk prays beside a stone Buddha in Sri Lanka.*

## India

The British East India Company (founded in 1600) found it difficult to compete with the Dutch in Southeast Asia, so turned its attention to India. The company was granted trade concessions by Mughal rulers, dealing mainly in cotton and other textiles. Its monopoly was challenged by others, including the French, who were defeated in the mid-18th century. Later, the company's tea imports from China were financed by opium exports from India.

*This painting shows the British commander Lord Cornwallis receiving Tipu Sultan's young sons as hostages at Seringapatam in 1792. The Mysore ruler was forced to give up half his territory.*

## THE EUROPEAN IMPACT

**1482**
*The Portuguese build a trading post at Elmina on the Gulf of Guinea in West Africa.*

**1565**
*The Spanish establish their first settlement in the Philippines, at Cebu.*

**1612**
*The British East India Company defeats the Portuguese in India and wins trading concessions from the Mughal Empire.*

**1623**
*The Amboina Massacre underlines Dutch dominance in the Spice Islands (Moluccas).*

**1756**
*Incident of the Black Hole of Calcutta, in which it is alleged the Nawab of Bengal confines British soldiers.*

**1757**
*Robert Clive (1725–74) of the British East India Company defeats the French in India, leading to British control of Bengal.*

**1773**
*The British East India Company obtains a monopoly of the production and sale of opium in Bengal (for export to China).*

**1782–99**
*Tipu Sultan rules the southern Indian state of Mysore and defends it against the British.*

**1805–06**
*Mungo Park's second Niger expedition; he drowns when attacked by Africans.*

# Glossary

**Ascetics** People who live very simply and deny themselves worldly comforts and pleasures, usually for religious reasons.

**Basin** A low-lying, roughly bowl-shaped area of land which is drained by a river and its streams.

**Buddhism** A religion based on the teachings of Buddha (c. 566–480 BCE). Buddhists believe that human beings face endless reincarations (rebirths and deaths) unless they gain release through wisdom and peace.

**Bushido** The Japanese samurai's code of honor, which was influenced by Buddhism. The main rule was to be willing to die at any moment in the service of one's lord.

**Castes** The hereditary classes that make up the social divisions of Hindu society in India. Members of a caste can marry only people within the same caste, and they each have a traditional occupation that comes to them as a birthright of their caste. There are thousands and thousands of castes in India today.

**Caravan** A company of traders traveling together, usually with a train of camels, through the desert or along the Silk Road. The caravan was the safest means of transporting goods across Asia or the Sahara Desert.

**Ceramic** A hard, breakable material made by firing clay in an oven. Some of the finest works of art of Medieval Southeast Asia and China were works of ceramics, such as plates or vases.

**City-states** Independent cities that govern themselves through a council or a ruling family.

**Clan** A group of people belonging to the same tribe who are related or share a common mythical ancestor. Clans are often thought to have an animal founder and there are many examples of bear clans, eagle clans, and the like.

**Coptic** An Afro-Asiatic language, written in the Greek alphabet. Also, anything that relates to the Coptic Church, an ancient Christian Church in Egypt.

**Confucianism** The philosophy of the Chinese thinker Confucius (551–479 BCE), which emphasizes education, respect for ancestors, and a well-ordered society.

**Dynasty** A line of rulers coming from the same family, or a period during which they reign.

**Ebony** The hard, dark wood found in tropical trees, much prized for its use in delicate carvings and furniture.

**Envoy** A messenger sent by a government on a special mission and who acts as a representative of the government or state.

**Exile** The condition of having been forced to leave one's homeland.

**Figurine** A small statue.

**Hinduism** The main religion of India, which involves the worship of many gods, a belief in reincarnation (being born again in another life), and a caste system.

**Iron Age** The period in human development following the Bronze Age in which people used iron to make weapons and tools. One of the Metal Ages.

**Ivory** The teeth of certain mammals. Elephant ivory is the most abundant form, from the long, external upper incisors of the animal, commonly called tusks. Ivory is a very dense, usually whitish material that is easily carved and worked.

**Jainism** An ancient Indian religion, with its own scriptures.

**Kasbah** A kind of medina, Islamic city, or fortress. It was the place for the local leader to live and functioned as a defense when the city was under attack. A kasbah has high walls which usually have no windows. Sometimes, they were built on the top of hill to make them easier to defend.

**Missionaries** A member of a religion who works to convert those who do not share the missionary's faith.

**Monolith** A statue, obelisk, or a column carved from a huge block of stone.

**Mosque** A Muslim place of worship.

**Mother-of-pearl** The hard, shiny substance found inside the shells of certain mollusks, such as the oyster. Mother-of-pearl can be carved into fine objects or inlaid into furniture.

**Muslims** Followers of the religion of Islam who worship one God and honor the Prophet Muhammad.

**Nomadic** Term used to describe a member of a tribe who travels from place to place in search of pasture for animals. A person who wanders and does not settle down in any particular place.

**No Theater** No or Nōgakuis a major form of classic Japanese musical drama that has been performed since the 14th century.

**Shinto** The name of the native religion of Japan. Believers worship a number of gods, from whom the emperor is thought to be descended.

**Sikhism** Sikhism is a religious philosophy founded on the teachings of Nanak and nine successive gurus in 15th century northern India. Sikhism originated from the word Sikh, which in turn comes from the Sanskrit root *śiṣya* meaning "disciple" or "learner."

**Shogun** A Japanese hereditary military dictator who had greater power than the emperor.

**Subcontinent** A subcontinent is a large, relatively self-contained landmass forming a subdivision of a continent. The word Subcontinent, used on its own in English, commonly means the Indian subcontinent (South Asia).

**Sultan** A royal ruler of a Muslim country.

**Sultanate** The dynasty and lands ruled by a sultan.

**Taoism** A popular Chinese philosophy that argues for a simple, honest life and the noninterference in the course of natural events.

**Terra-cotta** Hard, unglazed earthenware, made from clay. Early cultures made pottery and sculpture from terra-cotta.

**Typhoon** A violent tropical storm, especially in the China seas. The word comes from the Chinese words *tai*, meaning "great," and *fung*, meaning "wind."

**Warlord** A person with military power over a given territory that has no central authority. Warlords enforce their power by threatening or actually making war.

# Index